Facing the Long War:
Factors That Lead Soldiers to Stay in the Army During Persistent Conflict

A Monograph

by

MAJ Jonathan T. Petty

United States Army

School of Advanced Military Studies

United States Army Command and General Staff College

Fort Leavenworth, Kansas

AY 2011

Abstract

FACING THE LONG WAR: FACTORS THAT LEAD SOLDIERS TO STAY IN THE ARMY DURING PERSISTENT CONFLICT by MAJ Jonathan T. Petty, U.S. Army, 59 pages.

The purpose of the monograph is to explore the trends in retention during the last fifteen years during an era of persistent conflict. Frequent deployments influence soldiers' retention decisions. Based on extensive research from surveys, focus groups, and retention analysis, eight factors stand out. The eight primary retention factors for U.S. Army soldiers are family support, military and civilian education, quality physical and mental health services, pay and benefits, serving a higher purpose, resilience to adversity, realistic expectations, and leadership.

Each factor affects soldiers' perception of quality of life. This monograph makes several recommendations to commanders regarding how to approach retention during the long war. The long war refers to OPERATION ENDURING FREEDOM, OPERATION IRAQI FREEDOM, and other ongoing extended operations in the fight against terrorism and promotion of long-term stability.

Table of Contents

List of Figures

Introduction

In 2003, two soldiers fighting in Afghanistan discussed their future in the Army. They both served in their first term of enlistment and on their first deployment, but they held varying perspectives on their plans for future military service. The first soldier – anxious to advance in rank – planned to reenlist, gain additional training, and attend the promotion board. The second soldier, frustrated by the Army and deployment experience, swore he would never reenlist. Upon redeployment, the second soldier returned home to his wife and new child, finished his initial term of service, and left the Army. By contrast, the first soldier reenlisted, received the promotion he desired, and decided to make the Army his profession.

These two soldiers in Afghanistan serve as a broad representation of soldiers across the Army facing the reality of deployments. The second soldier, who intended to leave the service as soon as possible, simply stated that he could not accept the hardship created by a deployment and family separation. He felt he could never bring himself to volunteer to deploy again. It seemed obvious to him that the operations in Afghanistan would last an extended period— perhaps most of his career. He did not want to deploy for a year every two or three years.

The following analysis seeks to determine what factors, during the ongoing "era of persistent conflict" over the last fifteen years, have encouraged soldiers to stay in the Army. This analysis involves several related issues: the reasons soldiers choose to stay in the Army today or leave the service, the effect of multiple deployments on retention trends, and the relationship of retention and soldier quality of life. Finally, analysis of these issues should identify actions other than merely offering monetary incentives that the Army can take to increase retention rates.[1]

This monograph will show that in the last fifteen years, during an era of persistent conflict, several factors play a recurring role in soldiers' decisions to stay in the Army beyond their initial commitment. Reasons for deciding to stay in or depart the Army depend on a unique set of circumstances for each soldier.[2] However, one can identify retention patterns, or trends, specific to each era in the Army's history. This monograph explores the trends observed over the last fifteen years to explain the relationship between the current era of persistent conflict and

---

[1] Retention is the rate at which military personnel "voluntarily choose to stay in the military after their original obligated term of service has ended." See Lawrence Kapp, "Recruiting and Retention: An Overview of FY2005 and FY2006 Results for Active and Reserve Component Enlisted Personnel," (Washington, DC: Congressional Research Service, 2008), CRS-8.

[2] Throughout this monograph, "soldier" refers to all soldiers including enlisted personnel, warrant officers, and commissioned officers.

retention.[3] Its findings should help others understand factors that increase the likelihood of retention and the interrelationships between these factors. Understanding these factors will assist the Army in identifying desirable characteristics of potential recruits, reviewing current retention policies, and helping soldiers and commanders address quality of life issues while preparing for ongoing deployments.[4]

Primary Retention Factors

Analysis of Army retention during the last fifteen years reveals eight primary factors that positively affect soldier retention: family support, military and civilian education, quality physical and mental health services, pay and benefits, serving a higher purpose, resilience to adversity, realistic expectations, and leadership.[5] Each factor improves a soldier's quality of life, increasing the likelihood that a particular soldier will remain in the Army.[6] An examination of the relationship between each factor and soldier retention reveals that the factors are interdependent variables, which overlap and reinforce each other. Despite the overlap, each factor merits analysis in its own right, and in relation to the others.

Methodology and Limitations

Three major steps facilitate identification and examination of the factors that encourage soldiers to stay in the Army. Analysis of deployment and retention studies from the last fifteen years reveals the unique retention dynamics during a period of high Army operational tempo (OPTEMPO). The findings of research described in a wide variety of sources enable identification and analysis of each primary factor that promotes soldier retention. Finally, analysis of the conclusions drawn from cited research enables identification of several implications for the

---

[3] Trends of retention from other periods may have similar characteristics as the last 15 years. However, it is instructive for the future Army to look at today's trends.

[4] RAND Corporation, *Research Brief: Military Reenlistment and Deployment During the War on Terrorism* (Santa Monica, CA: RAND Corporation, 2009), 2.

[5] The Army Values are Loyalty, Duty, Respect, Selfless Service, Honor, Integrity, and Personal Courage.

[6] J.D. Leipold, "SMA to Congress: Army Improving Quality of Life," *www.army.mil news*, February 7, 2008, http://www.army.mil/-news/2008/02/07/7341-sma-to-congress-army-improving-quality-of-life/ (accessed December 29, 2010). Testimony given to the new 109th Congress House Subcommittee on Military Quality of Life and Veterans' Affairs. Sergeant Major of the Army (SMA) Kenneth O. Preston linked retention and quality of life in testimony to Congress. While SMA Preston spoke specifically about the Child Development and Youth Services programs, the testimony underscores the overall connection between quality of life and retention. However, not every quality of life measure has a substantial impact on retention.

Army's future retention efforts. The resulting conclusions provide the basis for several recommendations to change existing Army retention policy.[7]

While the foregoing analysis focuses on the United States Army, the findings relate to other services as well, especially given today's joint environment. In addition, this research does not explicitly address soldiers forced out of the Army due to Uniform Code of Military Justice (UCMJ) violations or administratively discharged for a variety of reasons. Finally, respondents' answers reflect intentions to stay in or leave the Army. Therefore, this paper does not tie surveys results to soldier administrative data, unless otherwise specifically mentioned.[8]

---

[7] While this monograph focuses on Army retention over the last fifteen years, it draws on survey data collected within the same period but include questions about the Army of the early 1990s. The oldest studies cited, dated 1996, reflect responses from soldiers who deployed to Operation Desert Storm and Somalia. See W.R. Schumm, et al., "Marriage Trends in the U.S. Army," *Psychological Reports* 78 (1996): 771-784.

[8] For example, administrative data from 10 Status of Forces Surveys of Active Duty Personnel made by RAND linked the respondent with his administrative data. However, post ETS data is not found in any of the studies. See James Hosek and Francisco Martorell, *How Have Deployments During the War on Terrorism Affected Reenlistment?* (Santa Monica, CA: RAND Corporation, 2009), xiv.

Studies by Factor	Family Support	Military & Civilian Education	Quality Phys. & Mental Health Services	Pay & Benefits	Serving a Higher Purpose	Resilience in Adversity	Realistic Expectations	Leadership
Hosek	x						x	x
McCarroll	x							
O'Connor						x		
Hosek 04	x						x	
Griffith					x		x	
Hosek 06	x	x	x	x	x		x	x
Lee	x							
Klian			x					x
Unandohan	x		x		x			
Hoffman	x							x
Nawrot	x							
Hosek 09		x	x		x	x	x	
Rush						x	x	
Asch 06				x				
Asch 08		x		x				x
Coolbaugh	x							x
Szayna 04				x		x		x
Kapp 07				x				
Szayna 08		x		x			x	
Kirby	x							x
Loughran					x		x	x
TOTALS	10	4	4	6	5	4	8	9

Figure 1- The chart above explains how the author determined the eight factors. It reveals the number of times each factor appears in the 21 separate articles. Family support and leadership appear the most.

Several important facets of the research supporting this study require explanation. First, it relies on studies of both active duty soldiers and reservists. While each type of soldier reacts to some common and some unique motivations, analyzing the factors in relation to both provides a holistic picture of today's forces (the "Total Force").[9] In addition, as U.S. Army Reservists and National Guard soldiers experience more deployments, the similarities in the factors influencing their retention increase.[10] Second, the analysis references a wide variety of sources, and each

---

[9] "Total Force" refers to active duty, reserve, and National Guard together acting as operational forces. For background on the Total Force Policy. See Department of Defense, *Managing the Reserve Components as an Operational Force,* Defense Directive 1200.17, October 29, 2008 (Washington DC: Department of Defense, 2008), 1.

[10] Lawrence Kapp, "Recruiting and Retention: An Overview of FY2006 and FY2007 Results for Active and Reserve Component Enlisted Personnel," (Washington, DC: Congressional Research Service,

source uses different research methodologies. The number and type of survey questions vary, as do respondent demographics, location, and year of study.

These variations produce vastly different responses, making exact comparisons of results impossible. Therefore, the following paper highlights overarching patterns in the literature that help identify the most important factors in retention decisions.[11] Third, the diversity of survey questions and methodologies does not allow a comparison capable of identifying the relative strength of each factor. However, in the more comprehensive studies cited, the authors identify the prevalent major themes. Essentially, this monograph synthesizes the findings of this diverse range of studies, looking for patterns and trends in their findings.

Assumptions

The argument that follows rests on several assumptions. First, the Army maximizes its return on the investment it makes training new soldiers when the best soldiers reenlist.[12] Second, most soldiers, if not already deployed, recognize that they will probably deploy in the relatively near future. Army policy directs Human Resources Command and subordinate unit personnel managers to fill tactical units first, use individual augmentees to make up shortages, track dwell time, and spread the responsibility of deployments across the force. Therefore, no soldier can count on avoiding a deployment indefinitely.[13] Third, economic fluctuations create incentives and disincentives to stay in the service. The national economic situation changes over time, but the Army always competes with the civilian job market in its effort to retain soldiers.

2008), CRS-9, http://www.policyarchive.org/handle/10207/bitstreams/19180.pdf (accessed November 19, 2010).

[11] See Appendix A for the complete list of individual factors.

[12] Ann H Huffman, Satoris S. Culbertson, and Carl A. Castro, "Family-Friendly Environments and U.S. Army Soldier Performance and Work Outcomes," *Military Psychology* 20, no. 4 (October 2008): 257. Since the promotion ladder forms a pyramid, the Army can't keep everyone – but they need to keep enough to ensure they have experienced, quality troops to promote, and don't have to rely on methods like accelerated promotions, or putting lower grade personnel into leadership positions early (i.e. E6 platoon sergeants).

[13] The Individual Augmentee (IA) Program has been in effect since prior to 2001 and has accounted for a portion of deployed soldiers in the last 15 years. However, the Navy and Air Force are the predominant services providing IAs, not the Army. See Chris Amos, "Cotton: IA Duty Won't Decrease Soon," *Navy Times*, February 5, 2007, http://www.navytimes.com/news /2007/02/ntcotton 0702 03/ (accessed on December 27, 2010). Dwell time is the time a soldier spends at home station between combat deployments, operational deployments (non-combat), or dependent restricted tours. See Department of the Army, ER Message Number: 06-004, Issued 01/04/2006.

Fourth, the date when the Army entered an era of near-constant deployments remains a matter of debate, but this study identifies it as the start of U.S. involvement in Bosnia.[14]

The foregoing also relies on one key definition: a soldier's "family" includes spouse, children, parents, or relatives who constitute immediate support to a soldier, regardless of the soldier's marital status. Finally, this paper does not address the effects of Army stop-loss policies.[15] Force generation during large deployments poses challenges that often require conscription or stop-loss.[16] Many soldiers affected by the implementation of stop-loss chose to reenlist (and in most cases, received bonuses), knowing they had no viable alternative. Because most studies monitor intention to leave the Army, not actual loss data, conclusions only measure intent.[17] Therefore, analysis of the use of stop-loss or conscription to retain soldiers exceeds the scope of this paper. Much like the studies cited, the following analysis focuses on soldiers' *intent* to reenlist or separate, regardless of the fact that some lack the option to choose.[18]

Summary of Research

The research data that supports the following analysis enables examination of forty-two separate correlations relating to retention, from more than thirty studies in peer-reviewed journals, interviews, and articles. Many studies reference multiple surveys. In the research, quality of life recurs so often that it acts as an overarching principle or predominant theme rather than an individual factor. Soldiers make retention decisions based on a wide variety of variables that affect their perceived quality of life, encompassing overall well-being at work and at home.[19] A qualitative study of these forty-two correlations revealed eight primary factors that

---

[14]Soldiers that deployed to Desert Storm, Somalia, and other conflicts are respondents, so the results reflect their experience in these conflicts.

[15] Grounds for stop loss are in Department of Defense Form 4/1 - Enlistment Contract, which states "In the event of war, my enlistment in the Army Forces continues until six (6) months after the war ends, unless my enlistment is ended sooner by the President of the United States." Officers accept their commissions under the same contractual obligation.

[16] Hosek and Martorell, "*How Have Deployments During the War on Terrorism Affected Reenlistment?*" 47.

[17] Ibid.

[18] Retention goals for the Army have been able to be kept much lower due to the use of stop loss, as stop loss can act as a "backdoor" draft.

[19] Quality of Life is "a broad concept concerned with overall well-being within society. Its aim is to enable people, as far as possible, to achieve their goals and choose their ideal lifestyle. In that sense, the quality of life concept goes beyond the living conditions approach, which tends to focus on the material resources available to individuals" Quality of Life studies became popular in the 1970s. See Jens Alber, et al., "The Quality of Life in Europe," *European Foundation for the Improvement of Living and Working Conditions* (Luxembourg: Office for Official Publications of the European Communities, 2004), 2.

6

emerged as consistent elements of soldiers' perceived quality of life and that positively affect retention. Appendix A includes the complete list of the forty-two factors considered in the study; the following paragraphs describe in detail the eight primary factors that emerged from the analysis of the research data.

Most of the research studies reflect the results of surveys of Army soldiers. The organizations that conducted this research fall into six categories: non-profit research groups that receive grants from the Department of Defense, for-profit research organizations, in-house military research institutes, U.S. Federal research services, private research papers written by civilian academics, and other books, articles and interviews. Many of these findings appear in peer-reviewed journals like *Military Medicine, Armed Forces & Society, Journal of the American Medical Association, Defense and Peace Economics, Military Psychology, Journal of Political & Military Sociology,* and *Journal of Leadership & Organizational Studies*. The primary factors, described below do not appear in any specific order. They consist of family support, military and civilian education, quality physical and mental health services, pay and benefits, serving a higher purpose, resilience to adversity, realistic expectations, and leadership.

Family support stands out as a central theme. It includes both the Army's support of the family, and the family's support of the soldier. Soldiers whose spouses want them to stay in the Army tend to stay in, as well as soldiers whose families successfully integrated themselves into the military community.[20] Families feel support when local commanders and other leaders focus on people, rather than programs, that create a family-friendly environment.[21] Leaders who exemplify selfless service, respect, and loyalty to soldiers and families create a sense of community integration, which leads to higher retention.[22]

Education includes both access to civilian education and Professional Military Education (PME) and training. Soldiers who perceive that they obtain and use their Army education in meaningful ways tend to stay in the Army.[23] Soldiers generally expect to receive challenging and realistic military training, which not only improves their capability as soldiers, but also leads to greater individual physical and emotional fitness.[24] Access to quality education and training

---

[20] Lolita Burrell, Doris Briley Durand, and Jennifer Fortado, "Military Community Integration and Its Effect on Well-Being and Retention," *Armed Forces & Society* 30, no. 1 (Fall 2003), 8.

[21] Collette van Laar, *Increasing Sense of Community in the Military: The Role of Personnel Support Programs,"* (Santa Monica, CA: RAND Corporation, 1999), xi.

[22] Burrell et al., "Military Community Integration," 8.

[23] RAND Corporation, *Research Brief: Military Reenlistment and Deployment During the War on Terrorism,*1.

[24] Ibid.

improves soldier efficacy, builds stronger units, and encourages personal development.[25] Efficacy

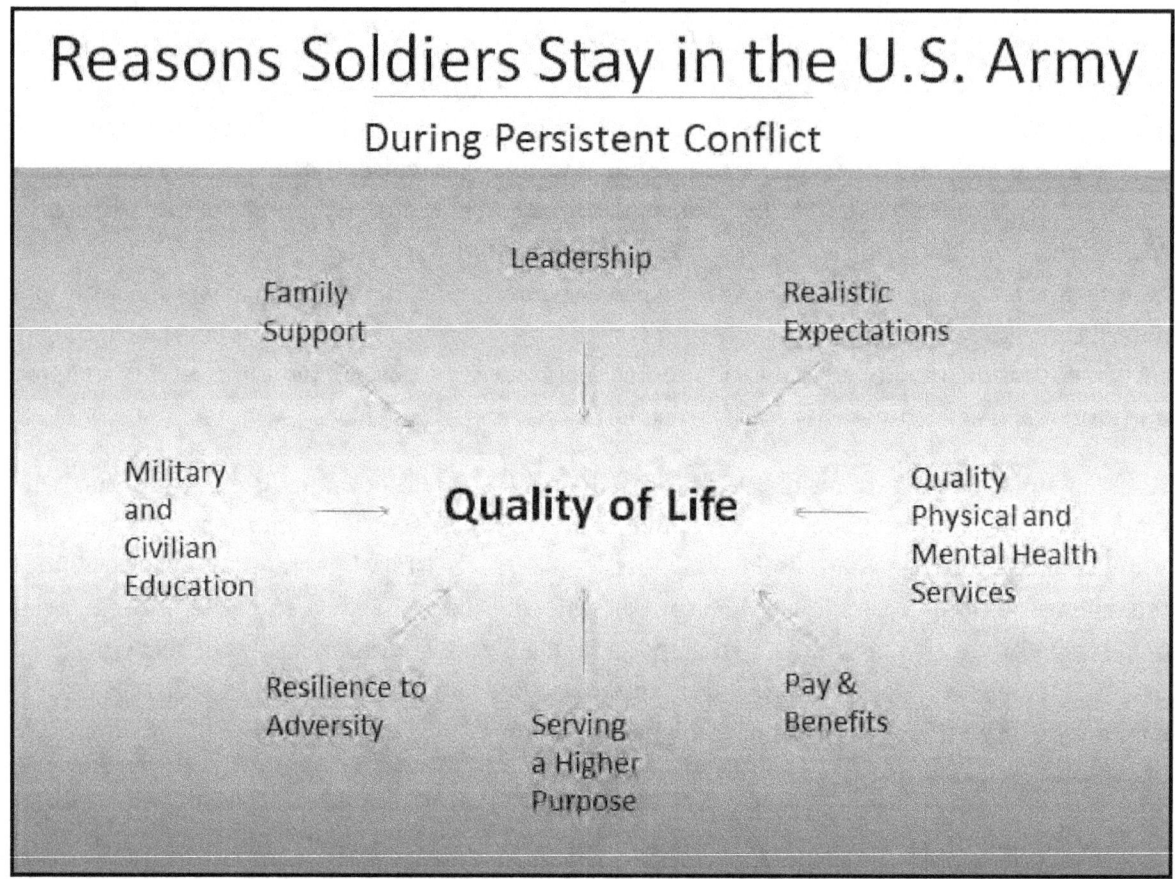

Figure 2 -- Subjective comparative analysis shows eight primary factors have influenced U.S. Army soldiers to stay in the Army beyond their initial term of enlistment during the last fifteen years.

also leads to a belief in serving a higher purpose as a unit or as an Army.[26] Civilian educational benefits can create incentives to remain in the Army, but they can create disincentives as well, sometimes encouraging soldiers to leave the Army and seek civilian employment or additional

---

[25] Hosek, et al., *How Deployments Affect Service Members,* xxiii. According to Merriam-Webster Dictionary, efficacy is "the power to produce an effect."

[26] Ibid., xxi.

schooling. Overall, however, education both enhances preparation for deployment, and corresponds to promotions and increases in pay and benefits, which improves quality of life. [27]

Soldiers rightfully expect access to quality physical and mental health services. Nevertheless, many studies indicate a general perception of poor health services during and after deployments exists in the media and among soldiers, leading to decreased retention. [28] Soldiers who complete multiple deployments more frequently suffer from physical and mental trauma and Post Traumatic Stress Disorder (PTSD) than those who do not, making them much less likely to stay in the Army. Health problems also decrease soldier resiliency, as sick or injured soldiers are less capable of adapting to harsh conditions. [29] Due to an increase in emphasis on treating soldiers with PTSD, the military has improved available mental healthcare for soldiers in the last five years. [30]

Pay and benefits, including bonuses, promotions, and extra pay for situations including hazardous duty and family separation stand out as central ingredients of retention efforts. During the last fifteen years, the Army relied to an unprecedented degree on pay increases and bonuses to maintain its all-volunteer, deployable force. [31] Higher pay and benefits increase soldiers' ability to provide for their needs and to support their families. Quality medical coverage serves as one example of the benefits that significantly affect retention. [32] Better pay

---

[27] The military has a long history of using educational benefits to attract and retain quality soldiers. The best example of this is the original GI Bill, passed in 1944, and updated as the Montgomery G.I. Bill (MGIB) in 1984. The MGIB helped pull the Army out of a recruiting and retention crisis in the mid-1980s. The latest version is the Post-9/11 G.I. Bill, which in many cases expands the benefits to all military members and their families.

[28] C.W. Hoge, J.L. Auchterlonie, and C.S. Milliken, "Mental Health Problems, Use of Mental Health Services, and Attrition from Military Service After Returning From Deployment to Iraq or Afghanistan," *Journal of the American Medical Association* 295 (9) (2006), 1023.

[29] Anna Kline et al, "Effects of Repeated Deployment to Iraq and Afghanistan on the Health of New Jersey Army National Guard Troops: Implications for Military Readiness." *American Journal of Public Health* 100, no. 2 (February 2010), 276.

[30] In 2005, Congress reported that the VA failed to meet 24 special recommendations for care for military members. Since 2005, the military has increased emphasis on optimizing mental health services, including creating a Defense Center of Excellence for Psychological Health and Traumatic Brain Injury, which sponsors multiple initiatives and focuses Department of Defense efforts. See U.S. House of Representatives, *VA Health Care: VA Should Expedite the Implementation of Recommendations Needed to Improve Post-Traumatic Stress Disorder Services,* GAO-05-287 (Washington, DC, 2005), 3. See also Stephen C. Bowles and Mark J. Bates, "Military Organizations and Programs Contributing to Resilience Building," *Military Medicine* 175, no. 6 (2010): 382.

[31] Hosek and Martorell, *How Have Deployments During the War on Terrorism Affected Reenlistment?*, xvi.

[32] Kapp, *Recruiting and Retention: An Overview of FY2005 and FY2006 Results for Active and Reserve Component Enlisted Personnel*, CRS-8.

equates for most soldiers directly to increased quality of life, partially negating the increased stress of deployments.[33] Bonuses override many other negative effects of military services, ultimately allowing the Army to meet its retention goals.[34]

Many soldiers who believe they serve a higher purpose tend to stay in the Army longer than those who do not. Service to a higher purpose relates closely to pride in serving and a sense of accomplishment.[35] Conversely, long periods of no deployments leads to boredom, complacency, and the sense among some soldiers that their service merely means a regular paycheck. The higher purpose may stem from a sense of national pride, as seen in increased Army induction and retention rates resulting from the increased patriotism and sense of duty among many Americans after the terrorist attacks on September 11, 2001.[36] However, after integration into the service many soldiers draw their sense of higher purpose more from their commitment to their peers than to idealism or nationalistic views. Whatever the source, motivation based on the belief one serves a higher purpose translates directly to higher retention rates.

Resilience to adversity plays a large role in the reduction and management of stress, which leads to the capability to adapt to harsh conditions.[37] Resiliency increases the perception of quality of life for the soldier, because it enables the soldier to cope more easily with the challenges of military service. It leads to mental toughness and the capability to adapt under pressure – attributes that both increase soldier retention.[38] Every soldier enters the Army with some degree of resilience. In most cases, army training and the bonds soldiers form in that training increase their resiliency.

Soldiers who enter the Army with realistic expectations regarding deployments, military life, frequent household moves, and family separations exhibit a greater likelihood of staying in the Army beyond their initial commitment.[39] Interestingly, those who deployed either more or

---

[33] Hosek and Martorell, *How Have Deployments During the War on Terrorism Affected Reenlistment?*, 33.

[34] Ibid.

[35] Hosek, et al., *How Deployments Affect Service Members*, xxi.

[36] Kapp, "Recruiting and Retention: An Overview of FY2005 and FY2006 Results for Active and Reserve Component Enlisted Personnel," CRS-10. The post 9/11 increase in retention numbers, dissipated after deployments to Iraq began in 2003. This retention trend bears similarities to studies of the 1990s, which revealed a spike in retention during time of war, but later declined.

[37] Francis G O'Connor, et al, "Medical and Environmental Fitness." *Military Medicine* (August 2010): 57.

[38] Ibid.

[39] Hosek and Martorell, *How Have Deployments During the War on Terrorism Affected Reenlistment?*, xiv.

less frequently than anticipated tended to declare their intention to leave the service at the earliest opportunity.[40] In addition, realistic expectations prepare soldiers to manage multiple deployments. Regardless, as deployment frequency increases, fewer soldiers declare their intent to stay in the service beyond their commitment, particularly when they spend less than two years at home between deployments.[41] Unsurprisingly, older soldiers tend to exhibit more realistic expectations than their younger counterparts do.[42] Overall, the older soldier displays greater maturity and demonstrates less desire to change professions.[43]

Leadership has a tremendous impact on retention. Leaders who live the Army Values create an environment that soldiers and their families' appreciate. Leaders at the local level have great influence on retention decisions within their units. Mentor relationships help soldiers understand and cope with the challenges of deployment and adjustments to army life. Effective leaders help decrease spousal separation anxiety.[44]

Background

Since the mid-1990s, the Department of Defense has deployed more Army units in support of national security objectives than any other service.[45] Conflicts and interventions in Bosnia, Kosovo, Afghanistan, Iraq, and other locations have placed a particularly heavy burden

---

[40] Sheila Nataraj Kirby and Scott Naftel, "The Impact of Deployment on the Retention of Military Reservists," *Armed Forces & Society* 26, no. 2 (Winter 2000): 261.

[41] Hosek and Martorell, *How Have Deployments During the War on Terrorism Affected Reenlistment?*, xiv.

[42] Burrell, *Military Community Integration and Its Effect on Well-Being and Retention*, 18. Older refers to the age of soldiers, however, intention to stay in also correlated with increased time in service.

[43] Ibid, 9.

[44] K.W. Coolbaugh and A. Rosenthal, *Family Separations in the Army* (Alexandria, VA: U.S. Army Research Institute for the Behavioral and Social Sciences, 1992), 92.

[45] As of October 2009, "more than 1 million [Army] soldiers have deployed since the beginning of the wars. These 1 million soldiers have completed 1.5 million deployment events, with 352,700 deploying more than once." During the same period, the Marines deployed 251,800, the Navy 367,900, the Air Force 389,900, and the Coast Guard 4,370 personnel. See Michelle Tan, "Two Million Troops Have Deployed Since 9/11," *Marine Corps News* 18 December 2009, http://www.marinecorpstimes.com/news/ 2009/12/military_ deployments_121809w/ (accessed 7 December 2010). Furthermore, the Army has held the primary role in combat deployments from 1994 to 2000, with 211,000 individual deployments. See Ronald E. Sortor and J. Michael Polich, *Deployments and Army Personnel Tempo* (Santa Monica, CA: RAND Corporation), Appendix C, page 1.

upon the U.S. Army to recruit, train, equip, and deploy soldiers overseas.[46] The resources required to prepare a soldier for a first deployment far outweigh those required to prepare an already trained soldier for additional deployments.[47] Likewise, the soldier with deployment experience usually possesses a qualitative advantage over new or inexperienced soldiers. Therefore, it serves the U.S. Army's interests to retain as many soldiers as possible, both officers and enlisted personnel, to maintain a reasonably high ratio of trained, qualified, and experienced soldiers.

Army senior leaders will benefit from understanding what factors increase soldiers' willingness to stay in the Army in an era of persistent conflict. More importantly, Army leaders should know what factors encourage soldiers to make the Army a profession, not just a single-term event. While the Army has relied extensively on monetary incentives to meet retention goals and reward those who deploy, money alone does not represent the deciding factor in retention. With the ten-year anniversary of 9/11 approaching, a timely review of existing research reveals trends and supports overall conclusions that shed light on retention factors.

An Era of Persistent Conflict and Retention

Today's discourse both within the Army and in the media describes the current strategic environment as an "era of persistent conflict."[48] This phrase appears with increasing frequency in military doctrine, education, speeches, and briefings. For example, one can find thirty-three individual references to it in the *Army Posture Statement* published in 2008.[49] The phrase also appears frequently in civilian analysis and commentary, influencing policy, budgets, and retention incentives. In response to the demands of today's long-term conflicts, in 2004 Army leaders adopted a cyclical army force generation (ARFORGEN) model to manage continuous deployments.[50] For soldiers, persistent conflict also means an era of "constant deployments."

---

[46] Thom Shanker, "Young Officers Leaving Army at a High Rate," *New York Times*, April 10, 2006, http://www.nytimes.com/2006/04/10/washington/10army.html (accessed December 29, 2010).

[47] The average cost to train a new soldier is $57,000. Much more if a security clearance is required. See Huffman, *Family-Friendly Environments and U.S. Army Soldier Performance and Work Outcomes*, 257.

[48] U.S. Army, *Field Manual 3-0, Operations*, (Washington, DC: Headquarters, Department of the Army, 2006), 1-1.

[49] Department of the Army, *2008 Army Posture Statement* (Washington, DC: The Department of the Army, 2008), entire document.

[50] "ARFORGEN is the Army's process for meeting combatant commanders' requirements by synchronizing the building of trained and ready units," said Lt. Col. Jeffery Hannon, deputy chief of the ARFORGEN branch at U.S. Army Forces Command. "By 2004, the Army was struggling to prepare enough units to meet the increasing demand, and ARFORGEN was developed to address that challenge." See Alexandra Hemmerly-Brown, "ARFORGEN: Army's Deployment Cycle Aims for Predictability," *U.S. Army*

This perception shapes their long-term view of the Army and their role among its ranks. If a soldier joined the Army after September 2001, and he or she deploys every three years, minus schooling obligations, the soldier will probably experience four to seven one-year deployments over the course of a 20-year career.[51]

A great deal of widely available anecdotal evidence leads soldiers to the perception that a military career means a life of constant deployments. After six years of fighting in Iraq and a surge of troops in 2006-2008, improvement of stability in Iraq led many to believe the pace of deployments would drop. However, in 2008 the government announced an Afghanistan surge would begin in 2009, meaning soldiers would probably deploy just as often, with only a shift in frequency to Afghanistan instead of Iraq. The perception may also be rooted in the belief that future conflicts will continue to be drawn-out operations. As the Army works to restore stability and promote democracy in various parts of the world, soldiers may begin to perceive these strategic goals as futile. All of these factors affect soldiers' reenlistment decisions. For some, the prospect of frequent deployments increases their likelihood of retention. Others see it as a reason to avoid reenlistment. For many, positive factors related to deployment mitigate a myriad of negative factors. Some will serve a single term and leave, no matter what the Army offers.

In 2006, General John Abazaid coined the phrase the "long war," referring to the Global War on Terror, while serving as the commander of U.S. Central Command (CENTCOM).[52] He used the phrase to emphasize that the U.S. faces an enemy prepared to remain "engaged in a generational conflict" and expected to fight for decades, not years.[53] This carries astounding implications for the U.S. Army soldier. The idea of fighting for decades means that today's potential recruits or re-enlistees may represent the first group of U.S. Army soldiers in history who face the prospect of serving in an Army that will remain engaged in combat continuously for the rest of their careers, and perhaps much longer. It makes no difference whether this worst-case scenario emerges as reality, since in terms of the topic of this study the important issue remains the individual perceptions that drive retention rates and career decisions.

News Homepage, November 19, 2009, http://www.army.mil/-news/2009/11/19/30668-arforgen-armys-deployment-cycle-aims-for-predictability/(accessed December 7, 2010).

[51] This reflects the ARFORGEN goal of a maximum 1:3 ratio of deployment to "dwell" time ("dwell meaning time between deployments). This ratio does not include time in Army schools and non-deployable duty positions. It also only reflects an ideal goal; some soldiers have experienced multiple deployments at rates as high as 0.9:1. Even soldiers in non-deployable units are subject to deployment as individual augmentees.

[52] Kapp, "Recruiting and Retention: An Overview of FY2006 and FY2007 Results for Active and Reserve Component Enlisted Personnel," CRS-12.

[53] Ibid.

Linda Robinson, in her recent book *Tell Me How this Ends,* cited a now-famous quote by General David Petraeus about the difficulties of leaving Iraq.[54] Despite a significant drawdown of forces and an increase in stability in Iraq, most believed upon her book's publication in 2008 – and still do now – that U.S. Army forces will remain there for years to come. In a 2009 report, *Building Security Forces and Ministerial Capacity: Iraq as a Primer,* Lieutenant General (Retired) James Dubik asserts that the Department of Defense must increasingly train its soldiers and officers to conduct Security Force Assistance (SFA) missions. He highlights six key findings in the report:

> <u>Future conflicts will likely arise in failing states</u> and will therefore involve the Army in counterinsurgency (COIN) or stability operations. The conventional forces of the United States Army will have an enduring requirement to build the security forces and security ministries of other countries.

> This requirement is consequently not an aberration, unique to Iraq and Afghanistan.

> The responsibility for defeating an insurgency lies with U.S. as well as indigenous forces. Passing on an active insurgency to weak indigenous forces is a failing strategy.

> Increasing indigenous security forces <u>reduces but does not eliminate</u> the need for U.S. forces in counterinsurgency conflicts and in the state-building efforts that follow.

> Building armies and the institutions that support them takes years

> Policymakers mistakenly equate developing indigenous security forces with an exit strategy from conflict, arguing that as indigenous troops stand up, American forces can "stand-down."[55]

---

[54] Linda Robinson, *Tell Me How This Ends: General David Petraeus and the Search for a Way Out of Iraq* (New York: Public Affairs, 2008), cover. The original quote came from a 2003 interview between then Major General Petraeus and Rick Atkinson, a reporter for The Washington Post. See Rick Atkinson, *In the Company of Soldiers (New York: Henry Holt and Co., 2004), prologue.*

[55] James M. Dubik, *Building Security Forces and Ministerial Capacity: Iraq as a Primer* (Washington, DC: Institute for the Study of War, 2009), 2. Emphasis in the original.

Such analysis, found in LTG Dubik's article and many others, strengthens the perception of long-term overseas U.S. military commitment to operations in Afghanistan and Iraq, and in future military deployments in failed or failing states.[56]

America's war in Afghanistan, begun in 2002 and continuing unabated through early 2011 has lasted longer than not only Vietnam or WWII, but longer than the Soviet-Afghan war in the 1980s.[57] Even a drawdown in troop strength means some soldiers may remain on a cycle of deployments to fulfill a potentially robust SFA requirement in both Afghanistan and Iraq. Whether a soldier joined the Army prior to 9/11, or came in afterwards, he or she understands the potential for persistent conflict and constant deployments.

Retention Trends Since 1995

While most units stayed in garrison in the late 1990s, Bosnia and Kosovo created a number of deployment opportunities. Army retention rates during the same period dipped below the Army goals. In Bosnia, the all-volunteer Army gained its first experience with recurring deployments to a conflict on a cyclical basis. However, the pool of units that maintained readiness for these deployments represented a small subset of the Total Force. Regardless, during this period deployments influenced soldiers' retention decisions, both positively and negatively.

The active duty Army met its retention goals from Fiscal Year (FY) 2000 to FY2010.[58] As of December 2010, the Army appears likely to meet FY2011 goals.[59] However, from FY1994 to

---

[56] The 2011 non-war defense budget is the largest ever at $550 billion dollars. Policymakers want the Department of Defense to help "contain China, transform failed states into stable democracies, [stop] terrorists, train various foreign militaries to [stop] terrorists, protect sea lanes, keep oil cheap, democratize the Middle East, protect European, Asian and Middle Eastern states from aggression, spread goodwill through humanitarian missions, respond to natural disasters at home and abroad, and much more." See Christopher Preble and Benjamin H. Friedman, "A U.S. Defense Budget Worthy of Its Name," *The Cato Institute,* November 18, 2010, http://www.cato.org/pub_display.php?pub_id=12582 (accessed February 18, 2011).

[57] The Soviet-Afghan lasted just over nine years. War started on December 24, 1979 and ended on February 15, 1989. See Lester W. Grau and Michael A. Gress, Trans and Ed., written by the Russian General Staff, *The Soviet-Afghan War: How A Superpower Fought and Lost* (Lawrence, KS: The University Press of Kansas, 2002), xxiii-xxiv.

[58] Robert M. Gates, "Secretary Gates on the All-Volunteer Force," lecture given at Duke University, September 30, 2010. *Small Wars Journal,* http://smallwarsjournal.com/blog/2010/09/secretary-gates-on-the-allvolu/ (accessed on January 14, 2010). Secretary Gates said that the Army did not meet its recruiting goals. However, retention efforts succeeded annually after 2001. The Active Duty Army also met FY2000 goals, but missed FY1999 goals by about one percent.

FY1999, the Army experienced a retention crisis, missing its active duty goals in FY1994, and again from FY1997 through FY1999.[60] Several unique factors contributed to the Army's retention problems in the late 1990s, including a robust U.S. economy, anxiety over the reduction in Army retirement benefits, and the ongoing cycle of deployments to Bosnia.[61] In response, the Department of Defense increased pay and bonuses in 2000 to close the gap with the civilian work force and to keep soldiers with critical, low-density military occupational specialty (MOS) skills in the Army.[62] The Department of Defense also increased educational benefits, targeted crisis areas, addressed a July 1986 decrease in retirement benefits, and adjusted special pays.[63] Among the targeted areas, the loss of many junior officers caused concern for the first time in many years. This was due, in part, to the robust economy attracting well-educated officers with high demand technical skills.[64]

The Army measures retention success in terms of meeting retention categories: initial-term, mid-career, and careerist reenlistments.[65] Officer retention examines year groups based on the date of commission. The Army analyzes each category separately to look for problems and predict future shortages. For example, in FY 1997- FY 1999 the Army experienced a crisis with midgrade NCOs and captains, losing many soldiers to the civilian workforce. In 2007, a similar crisis in captain retention prompted the Army to offer substantial bonuses to officers who committed to stay beyond their first term. Repeatedly, throughout the research on retention, the Army has viewed the problem as one of finding ways to improve the overall quality of life, usually relying on increasing pay and bonuses as the main solution.[66] When not enough experienced soldiers stay in the Army, the result is degradation in experience and

---

[59] U.S. Department of Defense, "DOD Announces Recruiting and Retention Numbers for Fiscal Year-to-Date 2011 Through November" (Washington, DC: Office of the Assistant Secretary of Defense (Public Affairs)), December 15, 2010), 1.

[60] Beth Asch, et al., *Military Recruiting and Retention After the Fiscal Year 2000 Military Pay Legislation* (Santa Monica, CA: RAND Corporation, 2002), xvii-xviii.

[61] Ibid.

[62] Ibid., iii.

[63] Ibid., iv.

[64] Ibid., 67. See also Michael G. Clark, "Where Have All Our Captains Gone?: An Analysis of Why Junior Army Officers are Leaving the Service," (Strategy Research Project, U.S. Army War College, 1999), iii.

[65] Categories include initial term, mid-career, and careerist. "Initial-Term" is a category of reenlistment objective composed of soldiers in their first term of service. "Mid-Career" is the category for second termers with less than 10 years. Careerists are on their second or subsequent enlistment, and will have more than 10 years of active Federal service at ETS or on their separation date. See U.S. Army, *Army Regulation 601-280, Army Retention Program,* (Washington, DC: Department of the Army, 2006), 138.

[66] The reference to quality of life is a prevalent theme throughout Army Retention literature.

leadership leading to a less effective force.[67] Therefore, policymakers must understand the causal factors that influence retention rates so they can shape future policy to maintain an effective all-volunteer force.

Overall, the Army has achieved strong retention numbers since 2001, in some cases exceeding its goals by a large margin.[68] While this trend may seem counterintuitive, given the high OPTEMPO, it does not lack precedence. Studies of the Army of the 1990s reveal a similar trend of strong retention during conflict.[69] However, a direct comparison to the early1990s alone ignores the nature of today's deployments which are longer, more frequent, and more dangerous. A threshold exists where the negative effects of high OPTEMPO overcomes the positive effects of participation in a deployment, such as a sense of accomplishment.[70] Evidence for the varying influence of short-term and long-term effects exists in retention spikes that occur after significant events like the capture of Saddam Hussein, or the announcement of plans to reduce numbers of combat troops in Iraq.

The Eight Factors of Retention

The cost to recruit and train a solider exceeds $57,000 dollars. Because of this, the Army and other researchers are continuously examining the current factors that contribute to Army retention. If the army can encourage a first term soldier to reenlist even once, they receive a dramatic 30-50% return on their recruiting and training investment.[71] Based on a subjective comparative analysis, eight factors are relevant to the last 15 years.

Factor One – Family Support

Family support is physical or emotional assistance to the soldier from his or her family members. Family support includes assistance from immediate or extended family. Family support also encompasses those people, programs, or policies that create a network of support around the soldier's family. Soldiers' families provide better support when they are an integral part of a cohesive military community.[72] This community becomes more important to the family during soldier-family separation, allowing soldiers to focus on the mission. Support from family

---

[67] Asch, *Military Recruiting and Retention After the Fiscal Year 2000 Military Pay Legislation*, xvii.

[68] Kapp, "Recruiting and Retention: An Overview of FY2006 and FY2007 Results for Active and Reserve Component Enlisted Personnel" (Washington, DC: Congressional Research Service, 2008), Summary.

[69] Hosek, et al., *How Deployments Affect Service Members*, 11.

[70] Hosek and Martorell. *How Have Deployments During the War on Terrorism Affected Reenlistment?*, xv.

[71] Ibid.

[72] Burrell, "Military Community Integration and Its Effect on Well-Being and Retention," 9

and friends are crucial for maintaining an acceptable quality of life. Retention often hinges on central questions. Who is caring for the soldiers' dependents? What happens when the soldiers leave the family? Who takes care of their basic needs in the soldier's absence?

Family support is much broader than a Family Readiness Group (FRG), or an on-post program. There is no simplistic answer to ensure soldiers and families feels supported and the family integrates itself into the cohesive community. However, research validates several trends that increase the likelihood of retention. This section will discuss three important concepts of family support: military integration, sense of community, and family friendly environments.

Integration into military life is a significant key to retention.[73] Integration involves establishing social contacts and support networks. Studies show a direct link between retention and military families who perceive that the military community has embraced them. Spouses less integrated into the military way of life report poorer physical health and greater levels of depression. They also report higher levels of smoking, drinking, and other addictive behaviors. Less integrated spouses are most likely to encourage their soldier to leave the military. With such pressure, a soldier is much more likely to leave the Army.[74]

Army leaders understand this dynamic and provide a variety of programs to support the family. However, programs alone are an incomplete answer. A 2001 study asserted that "the U.S. military has numerous programs to assist families, yet having programs are not always enough."[75] Programs cannot necessarily change poor morale or a poor command climate in a unit. According to the study, *people* change morale and command climate, not programs. This study concludes that people are more important than programs in helping families integrate into the Army.

Based on the study, the objective for commanders is to create a sense of community. When commanders focus on people, not just programs provided by the military, families sense the difference. A 1999 study reached the same conclusion about the importance of people over programs.[76] When commanders rely too heavily on programs, soldiers perceive individual needs as irrelevant. A program may not meet the soldier's real need. Based on survey feedback, family's needs vary and commanders should treat them accordingly.[77] While a commander

---

[73] Ibid., 8.

[74] Ibid.

[75] M. Secret & G. Sprang, "The Effects of Family-Friendly Workplace Environments on the Work-Family Stress of Employed Parents," *Journal of Social Service Research* 28, (2001), 21–41.

[76] van Laar, *Increasing a Sense of Community in the Military*, xii.

[77] RAND Corporation, *RAND Research Brief: Improving Military Communities* (Santa Monica, CA: RAND Corporation), 1, http://www.rand.org/pubs/research_briefs/RB7528/index1.html. (accessed November 19, 2010).

cannot and should not meet every need, relying too heavily on programs breaks down the sense of community. A sense of community needs to be the overarching theme, with programs subordinate to it.[78]

A sense of community includes five areas: group symbols, rewards and honors, common external threats, attractive military membership (pay and benefits), and community and family programs.[79] Effective groups developed strong narratives in each of these five areas. Groups with a strong sense of community discovered optimal group sizes, levels of influence, personal investment, and frequency of contact.[80] In essence, communities are effective when groups are not too big for participants to maintain individuality, have input, or receive personal attention. Likewise, communities are effective when groups are not too small to be effective, comfortable, or share responsibility.

The study also suggests that the Department of Defense (DOD) cannot purchase a sense of community for families.[81] While well-structured programs can enhance retention, these programs are "tools that can be used by the military to allow individuals to become productive members of the community."[82] Commanders should use these tools to encourage, not force participation. A sense of freedom must balance the sense of community. Efforts to create a sense of community can inadvertently feel like a loss of autonomy, decision-making, or privacy.[83]

Another broad conclusion from the study is the importance of incentives from the outside community, not just the military. The perception of quality of life depends on outside influencers. Yet, these influencers still affected Army retention. Other community dynamics, such as sports leagues, neighborhood friendships, church and service organizations, school involvement, and other activities create a strong sense of community, as well.[84]

Several studies looked at the creation of family friendly environments (FFE). In 2007, separate researchers examined the link between the perception that commanders and their policies are family friendly, and the soldier and spouses commitment to the Army. The study found that family friendly commanders and policies are predictive of retention. The study also

---

[78] Huffman, "Family-Friendly Environments and U.S. Army Soldier Performance and Work Outcomes," 265.

[79] van Laar, *Increasing a Sense of Community in the Military*, xii.

[80] RAND Corporation, *RAND Research Brief: Improving Military Communities*, 1.

[81] van Laar, *Increasing a Sense of Community in the Military*, 54.

[82] Ibid.

[83] Ibid, 50.

[84] Ibid.

strengthens the link between perceived cohesion or military family integration and intentions to remain in the Army. Soldiers are less likely to leave an organization that they feel treats them fairly and allows the "necessary flexibility to manage their work and personal lives."[85] Moreover, soldiers felt that family friendly environments helped restore some of the imbalance created by the heavy demands.

While senior Army leaders develop policies that foster FFE, local leaders and their policies have the greatest effect on units and families. At the local level, FFE increases productivity, job satisfaction, and organizational commitments, all of which buffer the negative effects of work-life conflicts. [86] Researchers found a positive correlation between a family friendly organization and efficacy beliefs. They also found a positive correlation between a family friendly environment and intentions to remain in the Army.[87] Family friendly policies, known to increase employee satisfaction, are prevalent today in and out of the military. However,

The Effects of Family Friendly Environments on

Work-Life Conflict

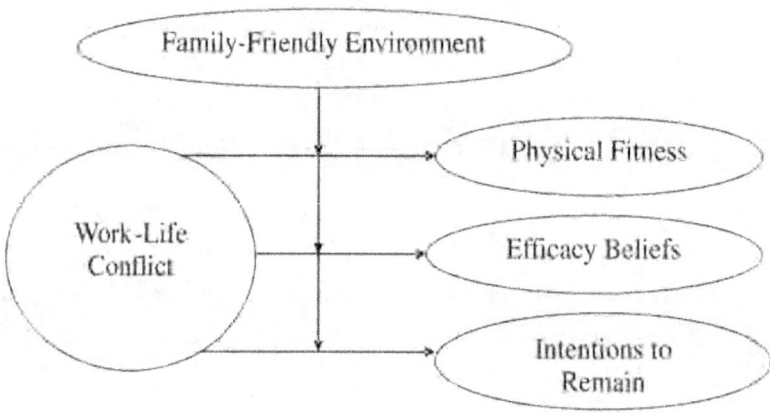

---

[85] Huffman, "Family-Friendly Environments and U.S. Army Soldier Performance and Work Outcomes," 264.

[86] Ibid, 255.

[87] Ibid.

Figure 3 -- The predicted relationship with family-friendly work environment as a moderator between work-life conflict and outcome measures. Family Friendly Environments increase intentions to remain in the Army.[88]

this study focuses on the specific policies that most affect military families and buffer against inevitable work-like conflicts, such as work stress, deployments, separation, and hostile environments.

Factor Two – Military and Civilian Education

The military places a premium on education and training. Broadly defined, education includes military and civilian education. Training refers to available through the DOD. Education positively affects quality of life and Army retention.[89] The Army creates multiple opportunities for soldiers, veterans, and family members to obtain education. However, some educational benefits, such as the Montgomery G.I. Bill (MGIB) and Post 9/11 GI Bills create both an incentive and a counter incentive to retention efforts, encouraging some to leave the military and take advantage of educational opportunities. Additionally, during persistent conflict, there are even fewer opportunities to take advantage of civilian education, increasing the number that leave.[90]

When crises in retention or recruiting occur, the Army immediately looks at increasing education benefits. The list of educational opportunities, in exchange for military service, is impressive. While the G.I. Bill grew out of post-WWII and the need to assist veterans, it continues to be a principle reenlistment incentive. Based on experience in the 1970s and 1980s, the Army also knows that increasing educational benefits can dramatically improve reenlistment, even though it may eventually hurt retention.[91] In 1980, the MGIB helped the Army bring in new recruits. The Army then used extensive Army civilian schooling and tuition assistance programs to keep them in. In the last fifteen years, the Army has again looked to increasing education benefits. Senior Army leader today have credited the new Post 9/11 G.I. Bill with an overall positive retention effect, because it allows soldiers to shift their GI Bill to spouses and dependents.[92]

---

[88] Copywright 2008, by Ann Huffman, used with permission from the author. Chart found in Ann H Huffman, Satoris S. Culbertson, and Carl A. Castro, "Family-Friendly Environments and U.S. Army Soldier Performance and Work Outcomes," *Military Psychology* 20, no. 4 (October 2008): 259.

[89] Shanker, "Young Officers Leaving Army at a High Rate." 1.

[90] Asch, *Military Recruiting and Retention After the Fiscal Year 2000 Military Pay Legislation*, 57.

[91] Ibid, iii.

[92] Army News Service, "Army Reaches Retention Goal with Fort Campbell Soldier" *Army News Service*, August 31, 2006, http://www.armywell-being.org/skins/wblo/dsplay.aspx? Module ID=f6c2 29ca-03ae-4c81-8d0a-81a5a 0c208f9& Action=display_user_ob ject&CategoryID=5b03 cbe2-1f7c-4d7f-bc2a-

Military education and training also affect retention. In many cases, the opportunity to acquire meaningful skills is an incentive to enter into Army service, stay in the Army, and depending on the skill set, to leave the Army.[93] Others stay in the Army due to unique skill sets applicable only to the military, creating incentives to remain in the service since those skills do not create civilian job opportunities. In the end, the Army has made a comprehensive commitment to educating its soldiers and officers, in order to improve the quality and effectiveness of the force.[94]

Challenging and realistic military training helps soldiers build long-term endurance and resilience to physical and mental challenges. The more effective and relevant the training, the more a soldier is physically capable to adapt, as well as able to reduce anxiety and fear when faced with challenging environments. Researchers have thoroughly documented the correlation between the reduction of mental stress and an increased willingness to stay in the Army.[95] Overall, military training is a critical stress moderator, and probably the most important single factor in reducing combat stress.[96] Not surprisingly, the study finds that "stress-exposure training, in which individuals or groups are exposed to certain types of stressors and asked to perform tasks under these stressors . . . can help provide individuals with accurate expectations of the types of stress they might face [and] teach them coping strategies to deal with stressors."[97]

These training events are not only critical to retention, but to soldier survival. Which type of training is most effective in preparing soldiers for current deployments is still in question. The military should continually assess and modify its training regimen to match current conditions. Shortening the lag time between lessons learned during combat and implementing them into training programs is critical.

Further research shows that service members value deployments as a way to use their training in real world situations. Military education compensates, in some part, for potentially lower pay to soldiers. Soldiers place a value on effective and meaningful training, increasing the potential for retention.[98] However, as deployment time increases, this value becomes less of a

---

0c5344090f60&ObjectID=fef014a7-fb05-4af8-b2da-687a110 4425e& AllowSSL=true. (Accessed December 12, 2010).

[93] Asch, *Cash Incentives and Military Enlistment, Attrition, and Reenlistment* (Santa Monica, CA: RAND Corporation, 2010), 2.

[94] Hosek, et al., *How Deployments Affect Service Members*, xix-xx.

[95] Ibid., xxiii.

[96] Ibid., xv.

[97] Ibid., xv-xvi.

[98] Asch, *Military Recruiting and Retention After the FY00 Military Pay Legislation*, 42.

factor. As addressed in the section on realistic expectations, this paper will show that increased deployment time reduces not only this factor, but also almost all of the positive retention factors.

Factor Three – Quality Physical and Mental Health Services

In 2010, researchers studied the effects of repeated deployments on mental and physical health. Based on 2008 deployment data, previously deployed soldiers suffer from Post-Traumatic Stress Disorder (PTSD) at a rate triple that of soldiers who possess no previous deployment experience. Repeat deployers also experience alcoholism and chronic pain at twice the rate of soldiers who have only deployed once, and they prove 90% more likely to score below the general population norm on physical functioning.[99] Those who experience multiple deployments also suffer the greatest risk of mental health problems. The Office of the U.S. Army Surgeon General has reported mental health problems in 11.9% of those with one deployment, 18.5% with two deployments, and 27.2% with three or four deployments."[100] In the research, previously deployed soldiers score significantly lower in almost every measure of mental and physical health.

In the New Jersey study, mental health measured PTSD, depression, inability to sleep, alcohol abuse, and drug abuse.[101] Physical health measures back pain, joint pain, and decreased overall physical functioning. Of the soldiers who participated in this study, many not only perceived health problems, but also had history of seeking treatment for those health problems. The study also revealed a significant underreporting of symptoms of PTSD and other ailments. The results showed that a significant number of physically or mentally impaired soldiers returned to combat.[102] While no direct correlation between decreased physical and emotional health and retention exists in this study, the data suggests that those capable of coping with decreased physical and mental health are more likely to stay in than those who have not. Because the diagnosis of PTSD, chronic pain, or alcoholism does not automatically disqualify a person for military service, the study suggests that soldiers who intend to stay in the Army long-term can benefit from programs that enable them to develop coping strategies for physical and mental health challenges.[103]

---

[99] Anna Kline, et al., "Effects of Repeated Deployment to Iraq and Afghanistan on the Health of New Jersey Army National Guard Troops: Implications for Military Readiness," *American Journal of Public Health* 100, no. 2 (February 2010): 276.

[100] Ibid.

[101] Ibid.

[102] Ibid.

[103] Ibid.

U.S. Soldiers should have the best health care in the nation. However, the number of soldiers affected by injuries, physical problems, and ever-increasing mental health challenges strains the U.S. military. The last ten years of combat has put the force at risk from the accumulative effects of a protracted war, especially in the area of available mental health professionals.[104] Army medical services and medical personnel are overburdened. Research confirms that the overall effect of poor physical and mental health is affecting the ready force, given the unprecedented pattern of multiple deployments.[105] The declining mental and physical health of the ready force hurts retention, as well as a myriad of quality of life issues. While the military lifestyle involves physical danger and stress, there are two broad conceptual approaches to retention. First, the Army can recruit new soldiers, break them, then recruit more; or the Army can apply a policy of taking care of those that they already recruited, trained, and want to retain.

Quality physical health care affects physical fitness, as much as regular physical training. Quality physical care is the only way to ensure the U.S. Army can endure the burden of extensive casualties, maintain a physically fit and ready force, and regenerate and revitalize soldiers who may deploy and fight during their entire career. Access to quality physical and mental healthcare means the Army can mitigate the risk of combat training, and take care of those who are in poor health due to multiple deployments. Quality mental and physical healthcare should enable the Army to retain, rather than replace, quality soldiers.

Studies also indicate that length of exposure to combat operations significantly increases adverse effects on health, and therefore negatively impacts retention.[106] Unsurprisingly, studies showed "separation rates from the military for those with mental health concerns are higher for personnel who had been deployed to Iraq and Afghanistan" compared with other deployments. Additionally, the need to address mental health concerns created by work and personal stress corresponds with the length of total months deployed.[107] To deal with the additional combat stressors, many soldiers turned to each other. Stigmas against talking with mental health professionals remain a problem. Therefore, the Army should seek ways to reduce stigmas, increase the availability of professionals, and teach soldiers how to help each other in the effort to reduce significant combat stress.[108]

---

[104] Ibid.

[105] Ibid.

[106] Hosek, et al., *How Deployments Affect Service Members*, 1.

[107] Ibid., xiii. Total months are not necessarily consecutive. The study uses total months as a measure. However, consecutive versus total months deployed may have different effects.

[108] Ibid., xxiii.

Post deployment survey data increases understanding of the relationship between screening results, use of mental health services, and attrition from military service.[109] Using 16,000 surveys from Operation Enduring Freedom and 222,000 surveys from Operation Iraqi Freedom, researchers found that combat duty in Iraq is associated with a high percentage of mental health service use and with decreased retention. This implies that despite the Army's meeting its retention quotas, deployments still negatively affected retention among those who required post deployment mental health services. The number reporting a mental health problem is 19.1% after soldiers returned from Iraq, 11.3% after returning from Afghanistan, and 8.5% returning from other locations.[110] Because soldiers typically underreport mental health problems, a larger pool than expected intends to leave the Army due to mental health challenges, whether reported or unreported, treated or untreated.

Quality health and mental services for family members can also mitigate the negative effects on retention. In one study, less integrated spouses into the military way of life report poorer physical health, greater levels of depression, increased smoking, and increased binge drinking. While the remedy in this situation is better military family integration, the importance of quality healthcare for spouses during soldier deployments is clear. Additionally, addiction programs, mental healthcare, and health programs for dependents need to be in place to best support the family.

Factor Four – Pay and Benefits

No other reason, perhaps beyond the Stop-Loss Policy, has had more effect on retention than pay and bonuses in the last fifteen years. During a period of frequent deployments, increased stress on families and potential danger for soldiers, Congress has repeatedly authorized increased pay, large bonuses, moving allowances, special pays for hazardous duty and family separation. Additionally, retention bonuses remain at record highs, and increased pay indisputably increases retention.[111] Incentive bonuses serve as central factors that contribute to soldiers staying in the Army throughout the last fifteen years, and particularly since the beginning of the Operation Iraqi Freedom in 2003. Bonuses can offset decreased retention, especially in relation to the negative impact of higher total deployment time.[112]

---

[109] Hoge, "Mental Health Problems, Use of Mental Health Services, and Attrition from Military Service After Returning From Deployment to Iraq or Afghanistan," 1023.

[110] Ibid.

[111] Armed Forces annual pay increases continue, despite an overall freeze on federal employee pay for 2011 and 2012. See Ed O'Keefe, et al., "Obama Announces 2-year Pay Freeze for Federal Workers," *The Washington Post,* November 29, 2010, http://voices.washingtonpost.com/federal-eye/2010/11 /obama_announces_pay_freeze_for.html (accessed February 21, 2011).

[112] Hosek, *How Deployments Affect Service Members*, summary.

Along with pay, intangible benefits have increased. Beyond education and health care benefits already discussed, the Army has improved family housing, barracks, forward deployed soldier services, daycare services, communication with deployed soldiers, internet access, time off, and a myriad of other programs and policies. Soldiers who once considered some Army benefits as luxuries now consider them requirements. Increased internet access in remote areas and improved living conditions serve as just two examples of these increased expectations.[113]

Hostile Fire Pay (HFP) and Family Separation Pay (FSP) help offset the negative impact from soldier deployments, increasing retention.[114] Research demonstrates that a point exists at which extending deployment lengths decreases soldier satisfaction at an increasing rate. However, a bonus can offset this effect, diminishing soldiers' likelihood to leave the Army. This policy, in effect during the 2007 surge in Iraq, offset the negative aspects of increased separation and danger. Adding to the benefit, existing tax law made bonus pay earned during extended deployments and reenlistment in a combat zone tax exempt. Further research should reveal how to best structure compensation models, but monetary compensation undoubtedly encourages retention even during extended and dangerous deployments.

However, extra pay alone cannot offset the negative aspects of deployment. One study concludes that family separation, high OPTEMPO, long work hours, and uncertainty from deployments represent some of the most negative factors for retention. Thus, extra pay proves necessary but insufficient to address retention concerns without additional incentives. Recommendations include greater communication capabilities between family and soldier, longer dwell time, regulated work hours in garrison, and better communication between the command and the soldiers to reduce these negative impacts.[115]

Retention depends on a series of decision points. The Army must consider soldiers' mental and emotional state during these critical decision points. Retention bonuses provide the Army's primary means to influence soldiers' reenlistment decisions during first term, mid-term, and careerist decision windows. Research shows that, without the stop loss policy, about one third of the soldiers who reenlisted between 2005 and 2006 would have left the service. Regardless of the policy, the Army paid record reenlistment bonuses to enlisted soldiers, even though they lacked the option to separate from the service. Soldiers with increased total

---

[113] In 2006, deployed soldiers started receiving wireless, highspeed internet access in their sleeping quarters on Warrior Base, Camp Liberty, Iraq. Also, a 2008 Army wide barracks investigation banned Korean era barracks after a Fort Bragg soldier's father complained. Both are examples of higher expectations of today's soldiers. See Ann Scott Tyson, "Repairs Underway in Barracks, Army Says" *Washington Post*, April 30, 2008, http://www.washingtonpost.com/wp-dyn/ content/article/2008/04/ 29/AR2008042902550.html (accessed February 21, 2011).

[114] Hosek, *How Deployments Affect Service Members*, xxi.

[115] Ibid.

deployment time formed a majority of the one-third who would not have reenlisted had stop-loss not forced them to remain on active duty. However, the Army also recognized the importance of reenlistments during deployments, and offered tax exemptions for bonuses received while deployed.[116] Additionally, commanders must ensure soldiers understand deployment pay, tax exemptions, and special pays. Helping soldiers resolve pay issues quickly and using emergency relief funds may also be appropriate.

Factor Five – Serving a Higher Purpose

Besides pay and benefits, many soldiers report the intangible benefits of continued Army service, such as a desire to serve others, a sense of team accomplishment, and patriotism. The common denominator is the desire to serve some higher purpose than *self*. The factor is service to a higher purpose: to friends, teams, units, or to a nation.

After 2001, the U.S. Army experienced a notable spike in reenlistments, based on a patriotic desire to serve during a time of war. Research shows that deployment can increase retention due to a sense of accomplishment, contribution to a larger cause, and opportunities to build strong ties with unit members.[117] These strong relationship bonds continued long after units returned and unit members moved to new assignments. Several surveys and focus groups confirm that patriotism and a desire to be part of the Global War on Terror had an important effect.[118] This factor appears throughout retention studies. A sense of accomplishment and unit cohesion are both important influencers for retention. However, these motivators have their limits. Based on one report, altruistic reasons for reenlistment are important, but insufficient for protracted wars. Because of this, the Army should cover shortfalls in retention by "increasing funding for advertising, number of recruiters, and providing larger reenlistment bonuses."[119]

If shorter, meaningful deployment time can have a positive effect towards retention, the Army can benefit from spreading the deployment experiences broadly across a well-trained force, rather than relying too heavily on fewer units and soldiers. When the Army relies too much on a smaller pool of soldiers, the result is soldier *burnout*. One study defines burnout as "long-term exposure to high levels of stressors or a single exposure to a very demanding event, leading to exhaustion, feelings of cynicism and detachment, a sense of ineffectiveness, and a lack of accomplishment."[120] Ironically, soldiers who suffer from burnout, even when they

---

[116] Asch, *Cash Incentives and Military Enlistment, Attrition, and Reenlistment* , 85.

[117] Hosek, *How Deployments Affect Service Members*, xvii.

[118] Kapp, *Recruiting and Retention: An Overview of FY2005 and FY2006 Results for Active and Reserve Component Enlisted Personnel,* CRS-10.

[119] Ibid.

[120] Hosek, et al., *How Deployments Affect Service Members*, 26.

accomplish the most, often believe they are not accomplishing enough. This condition can lead to PTSD, an illness that affects basic functioning and includes "nightmares, flashbacks, difficulty sleeping, and social isolation (feeling of aloneness, inability to engage in social interactions.)"[121]

Underutilization also has a negative impact. Insufficiently challenged soldiers feel a lack of sense of purpose. As discussed in factor three, effective training can mitigate this effect. Leaders must challenge soldiers, and avoid, when reasonable, from assigning mundane work to just a few soldiers. Closely associated with a sense of accomplishment, unit cohesion has a positive effect on retention. Surviving dangerous missions and working closely together in stressful situations has a powerful effect:

> We really had to draw on each other for strength—the people you were with all the time, the people you bonded to.

> You see people from all walks of life pull together. It's unbelievable to see it happen. All those personalities put aside for a task and you see them succeed at it.

> You become like family

These type of comments, published in the RAND study, *How Deployments Affect Service Members,* illustrate the close-knit, lifelong relationships developed during combat and deployment.[122] Anticipation of these types of bonds is often one of the major reasons soldiers stay in the Army. Conversely, once soldiers create these bonds, the desire to stay in may decrease, since soldiers had the desired cohesion experience and fulfilled this particular need.

Factor Six – Resilience to Adversity

Total force fitness, "a state in which the individual, family, and organization can sustain optimal well-being and performance under all conditions," has recently emerged as an area of

---

[121] Ibid.

[122] Ibid., 51.

study[123] Total force fitness centers on the concept of endurance – endurance of soldiers, families, units, and commanders during the long war. The holistic concept also addresses "every aspect of the warfighter's health and performance," including personal resilience and psychological strength against the effects of multiple deployments, PTSD, and suicide.[124] Total force fitness seeks to build physical, mental, emotional, and spiritual reserves to manage the stressors of Army life.[125]

Total force fitness includes medical and environmental fitness. Medical fitness, "a condition of mental and physical well-being," serves the goal of determining "whether an individual warfighter is fit to perform his or her job without risk to himself or others and to ascertain whether the warfighter has the physiological and psychological capacities to adapt to their specific occupational environment."[126] Medical fitness accounts for service and Military Occupational Specialty (MOS) specific requirements. It addresses overall wellness, immunizations, behavioral and disease risk factors, chemoprophylaxis, and personal protection.[127]

The second component, environmental fitness, provides "the ability to perform mission-specific duties in any environment and withstand the multiple stressors of deployment and war."[128] Leaders can usually identify these prior to deployment – they include heat, cold, ultrafine particulate matter, altitude, ionizing radiation, noise, hazardous chemicals, or biological agents in food or water.[129] Soldier readiness has a positive impact on retention due to reduction in stress moderated by the ability to adapt to harsh, demanding environments. Stress, when left unmanaged, negatively impacts retention.[130] These two components, medical and environmental fitness, are components of total fitness. Medically and environmentally fit soldiers can discriminate between those who can perform effectively, those who cannot, and

---

[123] Francis G O'Connor, et al., "Medical and Environmental Fitness," *Military Medicine* (August 2010): 57.

[124] Ibid.

[125] Comprehensive Soldier Fitness (CSF), an Army Program, currently addresses this concept.

[126] O'Connor,"Medical and Environmental Fitness," 57.

[127] Ibid; Chemoprophylaxis is the "administration of a medicine or chemical agent with the purpose of disease prevention, such as the use of antimicrobial drugs to prevent the acquisition of pathogens in an endemic area or to prevent their spread from one body area to another.' *Mosby's Medical Dictionary*, 8th edition, 2009.

[128] O'Connor, "Medical and Environmental Fitness," 57.

[129] Ibid., 58.

[130] Hoge, *Mental Health Problems,* 1023; Kapp, *Recruiting and Retention: An overview of FY2008 and FY2009 Results,* 12; Hosek, *How Deployments Affect Service Members,* xiii.

those who represent a potential threat to themselves and other soldiers. Increased total fitness leads to decreased disease, non-battle injury, and overall theater evacuations.

Combat stress reduction can come from several factors: physical fitness, challenging training, education, operational experience, functional support networks, and post combat decompression designed to relieve stress.[131] Understanding how to reduce stress forms part of the resiliency concept. The ability to manage this stress has a direct link to a soldier's ability to manage the effects of long-term deployments, as well as 10-20 years of military service. The Army should focus as much on prevention of combat stress, as on treatment of Combat and Operational Stress (COS). Each individual has a "breaking point" during combat. If the soldier reaches his breaking point, he can no longer function effectively. COS consistently appears as a precursor to PTSD, and COS training should be given to every soldier.[132]

The concept of a breaking point surfaced several times in the research. In his book *Anatomy of Courage*, Lord Moran compiles personal experience from both World War I and World War II to describe a soldier's struggle against fear. Unlike the language one finds in clinical studies, Lord Moran speaks a soldier's language. Nevertheless, he highlights factors common to modern concepts of total force fitness and combat operational stress.

Lord Moran describes courage, or willpower, as a moral quality that enables soldiers to confront fear. He describes courage using the metaphor of a bank account. In this account, everyone has a limited amount of courage. It can drain out slowly, as in sitting in a cold, dirty trench waiting for the enemy to act, or it can drain out quickly with a large withdrawal, like a giant explosion, "threatening to close the account."[133] In combat, a slow draining stress, or a sudden horrific stress can potentially push a soldier beyond his breaking point, affecting his ability to function. Courage serves as the antidote, and represents the same factor which may appear in the literature today as "psychological or physiological fitness." Lord Moran believed soldiers could replenish their bank account of courage through regular acts of self-discipline and will power.[134]

Whether the soldier thinks in terms of "psychological fitness" or courage, the concept of resiliency and a soldier's "breaking point" carries great significance. Long, drawn-out

---

[131] Kevin Broadnax, "Combat and Operational Stress: Minimizing its Adverse Effects on Service Members" Master's thesis, School of Advanced Military Studies, 2008. In School of Advanced Military Studies Monographs, http://www.dtic.mil/cgi-bin/GetTRDoc?Location=U2&doc=GetTRDoc. pdf&AD=ADA485474 (accessed November 19, 2010).

[132] Ibid.

[133] Lord Moran, *Anatomy of Courage: A Classic Study of a Soldier's Struggle with Fear* (Reprint, Garden City Park, New York: Avery Publishing Group, 1987), 61.

[134] Ibid.

deployments separated by minimal recovery time can cause a soldier to reach a breaking point. Sudden moments of punctuated fear and stress can have the same effect. The combination of the two over time greatly taxes a soldier's reserve of courage. This affects his or her willingness to maintain the ability to function, as well as their long-term intention to stay in the Army.

In the Army today, the long, draining stress, much like that Lord Moran describes, affects many Army soldiers. Research in the last ten years shows that while a single deployment tends to increase retention, second or third deployments have a negative impact. Soldiers with twelve months or less accumulative deployment time show a decreased ITLA. In comparison, those with twelve or more months (within thirty-six months of the survey) are less likely to reenlist.[135] This suggests that between no utilization and over utilization, twelve months of deployment time within thirty-six months represents the optimal ratio of deployment to recovery time. The one-to-three ratio of individual deployment to dwell time may represent an optimal policy, but the Army continues to experience difficulty achieving it, and this difficulty will surely increase if additional threats emerge.[136] The Army must also deal with the policy implication of finding ways to program bonus money year by year to react to deployment trends. The need to address mental health concerns created by work and personal stress corresponds with the length of total months deployed.[137]

Finally, commanders must prevent experienced deployers from denigrating or excluding non-deployers. Unit cohesion and morale can quickly disintegrate when new soldiers or non-deployers undergo hazing or unwarranted rejection by those who have deployed. The opposite of unit integration, isolating new soldiers, can cause unnecessary divisions in a unit.

Factor Seven – Realistic Expectations

Realistic expectation about Army service is an important factor for managing the stress of multiple deployments. Understanding Army expectations leads to increased retention. Likewise, unrealistic expectations about Army life, deployments, and day-to-day military routine can lead soldiers to get out of the Army. In a study created for the Office of the Secretary of Defense, RAND Corporation built a theoretical model to analyze the effects of personal and work stress, bonus pay, and number of months deployed on intention to reenlist and actual reenlistment rates.[138] With this model, RAND sought to predict how deployments and bonuses affect retention. The findings show that the number of deployments had the largest impact on

---

[135] Hosek and Martorell, *How Have Deployments During the War on Terrorism Affected Reenlistment?*, xiii.

[136] Ibid. Three types of dwell time exist. Individual, unit, and MOS dwell are tracked separately.

[137] Ibid.

[138] RAND Corporation, *Research Brief: Military Reenlistment and Deployment During the War on Terrorism*, 1

reenlistment, with negative effects for the highest total deployment time for soldiers and marines.[139] Based on the model, reenlistments decrease when the amount of deployment time either significantly exceeds or falls below expectations.

Interestingly, unrealistic expectations include not deploying enough, as well as deploying more than expected. To offset the negative effects of deploying more than expected, the Army uses extensive reenlistment bonuses for enlisted soldiers. Research shows bonuses can compensate for the difference between expectations and reality.[140] While bonuses help, commanders must also help new soldiers understand and prepare for the effects of deployment, separation, dangerous missions, and potentially difficult reintegration time after returning home.

The study sheds light on several aspects of retention. Based on the model, researchers predict that a decrease in OPTEMPO would increase retention. Additionally, as the surge in Iraq ends and OPTEMPO slows, there is a temporary increase in retention. This may be because soldiers feel that the toughest part of their service is behind them. Others suggest that seeing the size of the force increase, and the deployment ratio decrease is a positive step, but one that takes years to take effect.[141]

Before 2002, deployments represented a positive indicator of first term reenlistments. After 2002, the effect declined but stayed positive overall. However, by 2006 the trend turned negative. Second term reenlistments showed a similar trend. Thus, over time the accumulated effect of extended individual deployment time hurts retention. Prior to 2006, the break-even point for deployments having a positive effect equated to a cumulative deployment time of twelve months, with more than twelve total months having a negative effect.[142] After 2006, with sixty-six percent of soldiers already accumulating twelve months or more, the trend reversed to a negative overall effect. However, once the second enlistment started, soldiers better managed

---

[139] The theoretical model used in the study assumes that "reenlistment depends on expected utility in the military, versus best alternative." Expected utility is "home time, deployed time, and income including deployment pay."

[140] Hosek and Martorell, *How Have Deployments During the War on Terrorism Affected Reenlistment?*, xiv.

[141] Robert Goldrich, *The Military Draft and a Possible War with Iraq* (Washington, DC: Congressional Research Service, 2006), 1.

[142] Hosek and Martorell. *How Have Deployments During the War on Terrorism Affected Reenlistment?*, xiii.

expectations, leading to a trend in research data that demonstrates an increased rate of post-first term reenlistments.[143]

Based on the negative trend for reenlistments while still within twenty-four months of the last deployment ending, the study recommends a one-to-three deployment ratio to optimize retention and generate sufficient combat forces. Modifying current OPTEMPO to a one-to-three ratio accomplishes several objectives. With increased dwell time, soldiers experience less work-life conflict and enable them to take advantage education opportunities and other benefits at their home duty station.

Factor Eight – Leadership

Leadership directly or indirectly affects every soldier retention factor. Leaders influence unit cohesion, morale, community integration, promotions, benefit education, unit communication, training, and soldier expectations. Therefore, leadership as a separate factor requires independent consideration. One can hardly overestimate the overall weight and force of leadership on soldier effectiveness and quality of life. The U.S. Army defines leadership as "influencing people by providing purpose, directing, and motivating while operating to accomplish the mission and improving the organization."[144] Adopting Army Values forms an integral part of Army leadership. The values of loyalty, duty, respect, selfless service, honor, integrity, and personal courage are leadership standards. The following research shows a connection between Army Values and an increase in retention.

Research shows that effective unit leadership lowers spousal separation anxiety and results in fewer coping problems. Specific leadership skills include the ability to develop unit cohesion, communicate with families about Army life, and demonstrate concern for family welfare.[145] When these occur, soldiers and spouses perceive that leaders demonstrate loyalty to the unit and care about the burden placed on families during separation. When commanders integrate communication with families into their personal schedule, they demonstrate that they recognize family welfare as part of their duty. It also demonstrates respect for the family in managing work-life conflicts.[146]

Leadership can also reduce the negative effects of stress on soldiers. Research identifies effective leadership as a proven stress moderator that decreases the number of personnel

---

[143] This is most likely due to the effect of stop-loss and the incentive of the tax-exempt bonus. However, soldiers also better managed deployment expectation, based on discussions in focus groups.

[144] U.S. Army, *Field Manual 6-22, Army Leadership*, (Washington, DC: Headquarters, Department of the Army, 2006), 1-6.

[145] Coolbaugh, *Family Separation in the Army,* 92.

[146] Ibid.

losses related to job stressors. Tough, realistic training, unit cohesion, and high morale can temper combat related stress reactions.[147] Leaders also assist soldiers in their ability to build resilience to adversity prior to combat. Soldiers without stress exposure training are more susceptible to severe stress reactions in combat, particular when the target of enemy fire. Effective stress exposure training prior to combat helps build the capacity needed for combat.

Small unit leaders are particularly critical in creating unit cohesion and affecting soldier performance. The effects of cohesion are more intense in smaller units. During a crisis, "a cohesive group may be regarded as an optimal support system...because it provides emotional support, information, instrumental help, and companionship."[148] Leadership can greatly increase group performance by moderating stress. When developed, the right leadership attributes and skills can help buffer the effects of higher than usual stress. Skills such as effective communication and motivation, as well as the attributes of personal courage and selfless service will enhance group performance.[149]

Soldiers report a positive correlation between the intention to stay in the Army and the experience of leading soldiers while deployed. The opportunity to be a successful leader can increase retention, for both officers and noncommissioned officers. While correlation is stronger, however, in less stressful deployments, the study found that "deployment time is not unambiguously associated with...lower reenlistment.[150] When leaders have positive experiences in overcoming challenges in combat, they report increased job satisfaction and intention to stay in the Army.

In a 2002 study that examined the attitudes and behaviors of junior officers, the strongest single correlation between work environment and Intent to the Leave the Army (ITLA) was the leadership dimension. Specifically, officers who viewed their leaders as micromanagers, or as poor/inept leaders, were most likely to leave the Army. Other dimensions included problems with subordinates and peers, organizational challenges, equal opportunity, and antagonistic behavior.[151]

Young officers want to follow great leaders. That expectation, when not met, means greater junior officer attrition. Conversely, those who see their leaders as role models are more

---

[147] Ibid., 29.

[148] Ibid.

[149] Ibid.

[150] Hosek, *How Deployments Affect Service Members*, 11.

[151] Krista L. Langkamer and Kelly S. Ervin, "Psychological Climate, Organizational Commitment and Morale: Implications for Army Captains' Career Intent," *Military Psychology* 20, no. 4 (October 2008): 233.

likely to make a long-term commitment to the military. Leaders who actively mentor have tremendous influence. Leaders who train and assist subordinate leaders on how to act as role models, therefore, grow the next generation of leaders. Additionally, effective mentors that assist and guide junior officers throughout their career can also mitigate the effect of one or two poor leaders along the way.

Leadership and retention have a reciprocal effect on each other. The less quality soldiers retained, the smaller the talent pool. This creates less experienced leaders, decreased military effectiveness, and lower job satisfaction.[152] These conditions, in turn, increase the numbers that want to get out. Therefore, effective leadership assists at all levels with soldier retention, as well as overall military effectiveness.

Implications for the Future Army

As of 2011, the Army continues to meet its retention goals. This review does not seek to fix a broken program, but to consider retention during an era of persistent conflict and identify the primary trends or factors that encouraged retention during the last fifteen years. Understanding these factors will assist the Army in identifying desirable characteristics of potential recruits, reviewing current retention policies, and helping soldiers and commanders address quality of life issues while preparing for ongoing deployments.[153]

Retention trends adjust every year. Changing missions, the economy, and Army demographics mean that factors continuously fluctuate in importance and effect annually. Today, cyclical deployment schedules have tremendous impact on retention factors. Pay and money incentives will always be a factor. However, a thorough review of reasons for retention will continue to be instructive. Too heavy a reliance on bonuses may be insufficient in the future. As persistent conflict continues, the Army must adjust retention policy as budgets decline, missions adjust, and political, social, or economic factors influence the force.

The eight retention factors have important implications for Army leaders. Army senior leaders have an important role to play in designing policy that meets current needs. However, local leaders can be more influential than at the Army level. At the local level, leaders translate Army policy into orders, interact with soldiers' families, determine command climate, and affect soldier morale and welfare.

---

[152] Lawrence Kapp, "Recruiting and Retention: An Overview of FY2008 and FY2009 Results for Active and Reserve Component Enlisted Personnel," (Washington, DC: Congressional Research Service, 2008), CRS-8.

[153] RAND Corporation, *Military Reenlistment and Deployment During the War on Terrorism* (Santa Monica, CA: RAND Corporation), 2.

Army Values and Soldier Retention

Though not explicitly listed as a factor, Army Values serve as a common thread in retention decisions and appear as a central theme in retention studies.[154] Army Values represent a set of cultural norms leaders use to judge subordinates. Similarly, soldiers judge both their peers and their leaders according to Army Values. Soldiers who serve in units where they see the Army Values embodied in their commanders, leaders, and peers tend to have a more positive experience in the military. Leaders who instill respect and duty are more likely to build morale and unit cohesion.[155] There are also negative effects from soldiers who perceived their leaders lacked these same characteristics.[156] The perception of integrity, and honor, among subordinates is also a good predictor of higher morale and greater retention.[157] These values can have a multiplying effect, because they influences not only soldiers, but also peers and subordinates as well. Loyalty, which can create unit cohesion and effective leadership reduce stress moderators and increase the likelihood of retention.[158] Personal courage and self-sacrifice, antidotes for danger and stress, can help mitigate some of the negative effects of deployments.

Conclusions and Recommendations

Eight primary factors encourage Army retention during an era of persistent conflict. Research shows that soldiers respond to improvements in their quality of life and subsequently, the Army benefits from the retention of quality soldiers. At the local level, Army leaders should pay attention to retention before it becomes a crisis. Quality retention is a standing key task for Army commanders. Understanding how their soldiers think and what motivates them to stay in the Army remains critical.

Money alone is an insufficient motive. As budgets shrink, retention can become a crisis. Understanding the full range of reasons for retention is a far better approach. Leaders acknowledging all factors will have several positive effects. Besides meeting mission requirements, leaders ensure the best future Army possible by retaining quality soldiers. More than just retention, recommendations in this paper can help leaders prepare their units for the strenuous effects of deployment. The following list of recommendations for leaders can improve overall Army effectiveness and retention.

---

[154] The Army Values are Loyalty, Duty, Respect, Selfless Service, Honor, Integrity, and Personal Courage.

[155] Ibid.

[156] Langkamer, "Psychological Climate, Organizational Commitment and Morale: Implications for Army Captains' Career Intent," 233.

[157] Hosek, How Deployments Affect Service Members, 16.

[158] Ibid, 29.

Family Support - Integrate Families into the Military Community. Degrees of integration will vary for each family. However, work hard to integrate newly arrived soldiers, spouses of deployed families, families new to the Army, and separated spouses. Integration and a sense of community are important to retention efforts. Effectively use sponsors and mentors. Develop strong unit narratives incorporating appropriate symbols, recognition, and unit history. Encourage integration into the local community.

Family Support - Make Programs Subordinate to People. Soldiers do not reenlist as a group. They decide one soldier at a time. Consider individual needs and the effect on the entire unit. Empower leaders at all levels to focus on people, not programs. Avoid a one size fits all mentality. Educate new and inexperienced soldiers on how to navigate the myriad of available programs.

Family Support - Consider Family Friendly Policies. Before, during and after deployments, consider policies that assist soldiers reducing work home conflicts. Consider work hour policies that help soldiers meet family demands. Increase communication capabilities for deployed soldiers. Consider what gaps exist in meeting childcare responsibilities not met by local daycare policies. Encourage, without forcing, a sense of community.

Military and Civilian Education - Reduce Combat Stress through Tough, Realistic Training. Soldiers want tough, realistic training that prepares them for the next deployment. Consider which schools and training programs are most effective in preparing soldiers for deployment. Look into local Mobile Training Team (MTT) solutions, rather than only using offsite training. Take full advantage of Training Center Rotations to replicate stressful conditions. Focus on the reduction of stress through exposure training.

Military and Civilian Education - Encourage the Use of Educational Benefits. Help soldiers meet civilian educational goals while still on active duty. Educate soldiers on the use of tuition assistance. Encourage the use of the Post 9/11 G.I. Bill incentives for educating spouses and dependents.

Quality Physical and Mental Health Services - Reduce Stigma of Mental Health Counseling. Identify soldiers with PTSD early. Educate the force on PTSD signs and symptoms. Reduce the stigma of mental health counseling. Teach soldiers to counsel and support each other.

Pay and Benefits - Clearly Explain Pay and Benefits to Soldiers. Explain benefits to new and inexperienced soldiers. Use available garrison programs and benefits available to the unit. Maximize use of deployment benefits, pays, and bonuses. Ensure soldiers understand deployment pay, tax exemptions, and other special pays. Encourage soldier savings programs and use of emergency funds, as appropriate.

<u>Serving a Higher Purpose - Help Soldiers Experience a Sense of Accomplishment.</u>
Soldiers who feel underutilized tend to leave the Army. Challenge soldiers with important missions. Rotate mundane tasks among more soldiers. Spread deployment experience widely among soldiers. Maximize soldier readiness in the unit.

<u>Resilience to Adversity - Assess Total Force Fitness Among Soldiers</u>. Build resiliency among all soldiers through medical and environmental fitness. Identify and assist soldiers who have physical and psychological limitations. Help soldiers manage the inevitable stress of combat. Engage soldiers building physical, mental, emotional, and spiritual reserves to manage the stressors of Army life.

<u>Realistic Expectations - Help Soldiers Manage Expectations</u>. First term soldiers, without deployment experience, are at the greatest risk of unrealistic expectations. Once deployments and promotions occur, expectations usually change. Improve communication with the newest soldiers in the unit. Prevent experienced deployers from denigrating, or excluding non-deployers. Soldiers with two or more deployments may have exceeded deployment expectations. Assist soldiers with multiple deployments with needed counseling, personal time, and educational growth opportunities.

<u>Leadership - Reinforce Army Values Among Leaders at Every Level</u>. Leadership based on Army Values positively influences unit effectiveness, morale, and unit cohesion. Instill Army Values into subordinate leaders and soldiers. Encourage mentorship for each soldier. Courage and loyalty matter to soldiers. Honor and respect make a difference in how soldiers view themselves and the Army. Each of the Army Values can directly affect a soldier's perception of their quality of life.

Ultimately, leaders make the difference in retention. As long the Army remains an all-volunteer force, leaders will be responsible for keeping the best soldiers in the Army. The U.S. today asks soldiers to deploy more frequently than ever before. As the U.S. Government moves forward combating terrorism and enhancing global security, deployments will continue to be a reality. Understanding a soldier's motivations and intentions to stay in the Army will require continued critical analysis.

APPENDIX A: LIST OF ALL FACTORS

Contributing Factors	Researcher or Author. Date	Impacts on Retention
Community Integration	Burrell, Durand & Fortado, Mil 2003	Positive
Spouses Desire to Stay In	Burrell, Durand & Fortado, Mil 2003	Positive
Spouse Support of Soldier	Burrell, Durand & Fortado, Mil 2003	Positive
Higher Level of Core Values	Burrell, Durand & Fortado, Mil 2003	Positive
Pride in Serving in Army	Burrell, Durand & Fortado, Mil 2003	Positive
Older Soldiers[1]	Burrell, Durand & Fortado, Mil 2003	Positive
Years of Service[2]	Burrell, Durand & Fortado, Mil 2003	Positive
Family Mobility	McCarroll, et al., Deployment1995	Negative[3]
Deployment Separation	McCarroll, et al., Deployment1995	Negative
Physical Capacity to Adapt	O'Conner, et al., Med 2010	Positive[4]
Mental Capacity to Adapt	O'Conner, et al., Med 2010	Positive[5]
Overall Quality of Life	Kelley, 2009	Positive
One Deployment	Hosek, Toten 2004	Positive
Married and had Dependents	Hosek, Toten 2004	Positive
Reenlistment Bonuses	Hosek, How Deployments Affect 2006	Positive
Sense of Accomplishment	Goldich,Possible Draft 2002	Positive
Decreased OPTEMPO[6]	Goldich, Possible Draft2002	Positive
Increased Deployment Time[7]	Hosek, How Deployments Affect 2006	Negative
Mental Health Issues	Hosek, How Deployments Affect 2006	Negative
Increased Dwell Time[8]	Hosek, How Deployments Affect 2006	Positive
Work and Personal Stress[9]	Hosek, How Deployments Affect 2006	Negative
Longer Duty Days than Expected	Hosek, How Deployments Affect 2006	Negative
Sense of Community	Laar, Increasing a Sense of 1999	Positive
Focus on People not Programs	Laar, Increasing a Sense of 1999	Positive
Manage poor Physical Health	Kline, Effects of Repeated 2010	Positive
Manage poor Mental Health	Kline, Effects of Repeated 2010	Positive
Underused and Unaccepted	Dandeker, Royal Rifles 2010	Negative
Concern for Family	Dandeker, Royal Rifles 2010	Negative
Mental Health Challenges	Dandeker, Royal Rifles 2010	Negative
Family Friendly Environment	Huffman, Culbertson, Castro, 2008	Positive
Work-Life Conflicts	Huffman, Culbertson, Castro, 2008	Negative
Family Separation	Huffman, Culbertson, Castro, 2008	Negative
Non-Military Support Structures	Secret and Sprang, 2001	Positive
No deployments[10]	Hosek, Martorell, How Have 2009	Negative
12+ mo deployment every 3 yrsyrs	Hosek, Martorell, How Have 2009	Negative
12 mo. deployment every 3 yrs	Hosek, Martorell, 2009	Positive
Unmet expectations	Hosek, Martorell, 2009	Negative
Opportunity to Learn, Engage Skills	Hosek, Martorell, 2009	Positive

Contributing Factors	Researcher or Author. Date	Impacts on Retention
Meaningful Training	Hosek, Martorell, 2009	Positive
Prolonged Exposure to Deployment	Hosek, Martorell, 2009	Negative
Combat Duty in OIF, OEF	Hoge, Auchterlonie, Milliken, 2006	Negative
Reported PDHA Mental Health	Hoge, Auchterlonie, Milliken, 2006	Negative
Selective Reenlistment Bonus	Asch, Cash Incentives	Positive
Length of Reenlistment	Asch, Cash Incentives	Negative
Pay Increase	Asch, Military Recruiting & Retention	Positive
Educational Incentives	Asch, Military Recruiting & Retention	Positive
Career Opportunities	Asch, Military Recruiting & Retention	Positive
Bonuses	Asch, Military Recruiting & Retention	Positive
Separation with Soldier	Coolbaugh, Family Separation	Negative[11]
Frequent Deployments	Kapp, Recruiting and Retention 2006	Negative
Increased Bonuses	Kapp, Recruiting and Retention 2007	Positive
Increased Bonuses	Kapp, Recruiting and Retention 2008	Positive
Increased Frequency	Kapp, Recruiting and Retention 2008	Negative
Post 9/11 GI Bill	Kapp, Recruiting and Retention 2008	Positive
First time deployments	Kirby, Impact of Deployment 2000	Positive
Spouse wants to leave Army	Kirby, Impact of Deployment 2000	Negative
Overall satisfaction w/Army	Kirby, Impact of Deployment 2000	Positive
Neg. Psychological Climate	Langkamer, Psychological	Negative
Poor Morale	Langkamer, Psychological	Negative
Low Leader Commitment	Langkamer, Psychological	Negative

---

[1] Based on Available Administrative Data, not perception.

[2] Based on Available Administrative Data, not perception.

[3] It is hypothesized based on Burrell, Durand, and Fortado, 2003 that an abused spouse is be less supportive of the soldier in general, therefore more likely to influence the soldier to get out.

[4, 48] This reduces stress, which increases likelihood of retention. See Hosek, 2009.

This reduces stress, which increases likelihood of retention, See Hosek, 2009.

[6] Based on Available Administrative Data, but perception is still a factor. A decrease in deployment time may cause a temporary increase in retention, but it may not last in the long run due to adjusted expectations.

[7] Based on Available Administrative Data of total deployment time of 12 months and over, but perception is still a factor. A decrease in deployment time may cause a temporary increase in retention, but it may not last in the long run due to readjusted expectations.

[8] Based on Available Administrative Data.

[9] Multiple ways to reduce stress discussed on page 5??. Further study is needed to see if reduction of stress always equals an increased desire for retention. Hosek, 2009 suggests that it does, until the point the soldier does not see him or herself as useful, or feeling a sense of accomplishment.

[10] Research shows that those who do not deploy can feel a sense of underutilization. See Hosek, 2009.

[11] The correlation is between the soldier separated and the spouses desire for the soldier to leave the Army.

BIBLIOGRAPHY

Articles

"The Army National Guard Soldier In Post-9/11 Operations: Perceptions Of Being Prepared For Mobilization, Deployment, And Combat." *Journal of Political & Military Sociology* 33, no. 2 (Winter 2005): 161-177.

Bourg, Chris, and Mady Wechsler Segal. "The Impact of Family Supportive Policies and Practices on Organizational Commitment to the Army." *Armed Forces & Society* 25, no. 4 (Summer 1999): 633-652.

Bowles, Stephen V., and Mark J. Bates. "Military Organizations and Programs Contributing to Resilience Building." *Military Medicine* 175, no. 6 (June 2010): 382-385.

Burrell, Lolita, Doris Briley Durand, and Jennifer Fortado. "Military Community Integration and Its Effect on Well-Being and Retention." *Armed Forces & Society* 30, no. 1 (Fall 2003): 7-24.

Chan, Lillian, and Manny W. Radomski. "Coping With Stress from Work-Related Family Separation." *Wellness Options* no. 23 (December 2005): 25.

Cohen, Eliot A. " Book Review on Military Readiness: Concepts, Choices, Consequences." *Foreign Affairs* 74, no. 2 (Mar/Apr 1995): 148-149.

Dandeker, Christopher et al. "Laying Down Their Rifles: The Changing Influences on the Retention of Volunteer British Army Reservists Returning from Iraq, 2003-2006." *Armed Forces & Society* 36, no. 2 (January 2010): 264-289.

Drummet, Amy Reinkober, Marilyn Coleman, and Susan Cable. "Military Families Under Stress: Implications for Family Life Education." *Family Relations* 52, no. 3 (July 2003): 279.

Granger, Kay. "Military Families are Fundamental to Military Readiness." *Ripon Forum* 44, no. 2 (Spring 2010): 8-9.

Heilmann, Sharon G., John E. Bell, and Gavain K. McDonald. "Work-life Conflict: A Study of the Effects of Role Conflict on Military Officer Turnover Intention." *Journal of Leadership & Organizational Studies* 16, no. 1 (August 2009): 85-96.

Holmes, Samuel L., et al. "Military Physician Recruitment and Retention: A Survey of Students at the Uniformed Services University of the Health Sciences." *Military Medicine* 174, no. 5 (May 2009): 529-534.

Huffman, Ann H., Satoris S. Culbertson, and Carl A. Castro. "Family-Friendly Environments and U.S. Army Soldier Performance and Work Outcomes." *Military Psychology* 20, no. 4 (October 2008): 253-270.

Kirby, Sheila Nataraj, and Scott Naftel. "The Impact of Deployment on the Retention of Military Reservists." *Armed Forces & Society* 26, no. 2 (Winter 2000): 259-12.

Kline, Anna, et al. "Effects of Repeated Deployment to Iraq and Afghanistan on the Health of New Jersey Army National Guard Troops: Implications for Military Readiness." *American Journal of Public Health* 100, no. 2 (February 2010): 276-283.

Langkamer, Krista L., and Kelly S. Ervin. "Psychological Climate, Organizational Commitment and Morale: Implications for Army Captains' Career Intent." *Military Psychology* 20, no. 4 (October 2008): 219-236.

Maze, Rick. "Third time is not the charm." *Army Times* 64, no. 38 (April 12, 2004): 28.

McCarroll, James E., et al. "Deployment and the Probability of Spousal Aggression by U.S. Army Soldiers." *Military Medicine* 175, no. 5 (May 2010): 352-356.

O'Connor, Francis G., et al. "Medical and Environmental Fitness." *Military Medicine* (August 2010): 57-64.

Preble, Christopher A. and Benjamin H. Friedman. "A U.S. Defense Budget Worthy of Its Name." November 18, 2010, http://www.cato.org/pub_display.php?pub_id=12582 (accessed February 18, 2011).

Reed, Brian J., and David R. Segal. "The Impact of Multiple Deployments on Soldiers' Peacekeeping Attitudes, Morale, and Retention." *Armed Forces & Society* 27, no. 1 (Fall 2000): 57-78.

Schumm, W. R., et al. "Marriage Trends in the U.S. Army." *Psychological Reports* 78, (1996). 771-784.

Secret, M., & G. Sprang. "The Effects of Family-Friendly Workplace Environments on the Work-Family Stress of Employed Parents." *Journal of Social Service Research* 28 (2001): 21–41.

Shanker, Thom. "Young Officers Leaving Army at a High Rate." *NewYork Times*, April 10, 2006, http://www.nytimes.com/2006/04/10/washington/10army.html (accessed December 29, 2010).

Tilghman, Andrew. "The Army's Other Crisis." *Washington Monthly* 39, no. 12 (December 2007): 44.

Reports

Alber, Jens, et. al. *The Quality of Life in Europe*. European Foundation for the Improvement of Living and Working Conditions. Luxembourg: Office for Official Publications of the European Communities, 2004).

Asch, Beth. *Cash Incentives and Military Enlistment, Attrition, and Reenlistment*. Santa Monica, CA: RAND Corporation, 2010.

Asch, Beth, et al. *Military Recruiting and Retention After the Fiscal Year 2000 Military Pay Legislation*. Santa Monica, CA: RAND Corporation, 2002.

Hosek, James and Francisco Martorell. *How Have Deployments During the War on Terrorism Affected Reenlistment?* Santa Monica, CA: RAND Corporation, 2009.

Hosek, James and Mark Totten. *The Effect of Deployment on First and Second Term Re-enlistment in the US Active Duty Force*. Santa Monica, CA: RAND Corporation, 2004.

Hosek, James, Jennifer Kavanagh and Laura Miller. *How Deployments Affect Service Members*. Santa Monica, CA: RAND Corporation, 2004.

RAND Corporation. *Research Brief: Military Reenlistment and Deployment During the War on Terrorism*. Santa Monica, CA: RAND Corporation, 2009.

Sortor, Ronald E. and J. Michael Polich. *Deployments and Army Personnel Tempo*. Santa Monica, CA: RAND Corporation, 2000.

van Laar, Collette. *Increasing Sense of Community in the Military: The Role of Personnel Support Programs*. Santa Monica, CA: RAND Corporation, 1999.

Government Publications

Congressional Budget Office. *Recruiting, Retention, and Future Levels of Military Personnel*. Washington, DC: Government Printing Office, 2006.

Coolbaugh, K.W. and A. Rosenthal. *Family Separations in the Army*. ARI Technical Report 964 Alexandria, VA: U.S. Army Research Institute for the Behavioral and Social Sciences, 1992.

Goldich, Robert. *The Military Draft and a Possible War with Iraq*. Washington, DC: Congressional Research Service, 2003, http://www.fas.org/man/crs/RL31715.pdf (accessed November 19, 2010).

Henning, Charles A., *U.S. Military Stop Loss Program: Key Questions and Answers*. Washington, DC: Congressional Research Service, 2009.

Kapp, Lawrence. *Recruiting and Retention: An Overview of FY2005 and FY2006 Results for Active and Reserve Component Enlisted Personnel*. Washington, DC: Congressional Research Service, 2006, http://digital.library.unt.edu/ark:/67531/metacrs8290/ (accessed November 19, 2010).

Kapp, Lawrence. Recruiting and Retention: *An Overview of FY2006 and FY2007 Results for Active and Reserve Component Enlisted Personnel*. Washington, DC: Congressional Research Service, 2008, http://www.policyarchive.org/handle/10207/bitstreams /19180.pdf (accessed November 19, 2010).

Sticha, Paul, Paul Hogan and Maris Diane. *Personnel Tempo: Definition, Measurement, and Effects on Retention, Readiness and Quality of Life*. Arlington, VA.: Army Research Institute, 1999.

U.S Army. *Army Regulation 601-280, Army Retention Program*. Washington, DC: Headquarters, Department of the Army, 2006.

U.S. House of Representatives. Armed Services Committee. *Military Readiness: Impact of Current Operations and Actions Needed to Rebuild Readiness of U.S. Ground Forces*. GAO-08-497T. Washington, DC: U.S. Government Accountability Office, 2008.

U.S. House of Representatives. *VA Health Care: VA Should Expedite the Implementation of Recommendations Needed to Improve Post-Traumatic Stress Disorder Services*. GAO-05-287. Washington, DC: U.S. Government Accountability Office, 2005.

Books

Armstrong, Keith. *Courage After Fire*. Berkeley: Ulysses Press, 2006.

Betts, Richard K. *Military Readiness: Concepts, Choices, Consequences*. Washington, DC: Brookings Institution, 1995.

Cantrell, Bridget. *Souls Under Siege: The Effects of Multiple Troop Deployments-and How to Weather the Storm*. Bellingham, WA: HTH International, 2009.

Kindsvatter, Peter S. *American Soldiers: Ground Combat in the World Wars, Korea, and Vietnam*. Lawrence, Kansas: University Press of Kansas, 2003.

Moran, Lord. *Anatomy of Courage: A Classic Study of a Soldier's Struggle with Fear*. 1945. Reprint, New York: Avery Publishing Group, 1987.

Reivich, Karen and Andrew Shatte. *The Resilience Factor*. New York: Broadway Books, 2003.

Interviews

Lessard, Laurence and Timothy Reese. "Operational Leadership Experiences in the Global War on Terrorism: Interview With MG James A. Kelley." Fort Leavenworth, Kansas: Combat Studies Institute, 2007.

Monographs and Research Projects

Broadnax, Kevin. "Combat and Operational Stress: Minimizing its Adverse Effects on Service Members." Monograph, School of Advanced Military Studies, 2008, http://www. dtic.mil/cgi-bin/GetTRDoc?Locatio n=U2&doc=GetTRDoc. pdf&AD=A DA485474 (accessed November 19, 2010).

Clark, Michael G. "Where Have All Our Captains Gone?: An Analysis of Why Junior Army Officers are Leaving the Service." Strategy Research Project, U.S. Army War College, 1999, http://www.dtic.mil/cgi-bin/GetTRDoc?AD=ADA364553 &Location=U2&doc= GetTRDoc.pdf.

McLamb, Joseph S. "How Thin Is the Ice?: The Potential for Collapse in Today's Army." Monograph, School of Advanced Military Studies, 2008, http://cgsc.contentdm.oclc.org/ cdm4/item_viewer.php?CIS OROOT= /p4013 coll3&CISOPTR= 2546&CISOBOX =1&REC=1 (accessed November 19, 2010).